About Island Press

Since 1984, the nonprofit organization Island Press has been stimulating, shaping, and communicating ideas that are essential for solving environmental problems worldwide. With more than 1,000 titles in print and some 30 new releases each year, we are the nation's leading publisher on environmental issues. We identify innovative thinkers and emerging trends in the environmental field. We work with world-renowned experts and authors to develop cross-disciplinary solutions to environmental challenges.

Island Press designs and executes educational campaigns, in conjunction with our authors, to communicate their critical messages in print, in person, and online using the latest technologies, innovative programs, and the media. Our goal is to reach targeted audiences—scientists, policy makers, environmental advocates, urban planners, the media, and concerned citizens—with information that can be used to create the framework for long-term ecological health and human well-being.

Island Press gratefully acknowledges major support from The Bobolink Foundation, Caldera Foundation, The Curtis and Edith Munson Foundation, The Forrest C. and Frances H. Lattner Foundation, The JPB Foundation, The Kresge Foundation, The Summit Charitable Foundation, Inc., and many other generous organizations and individuals.

The opinions expressed in this book are those of the author(s) and do not necessarily reflect the views of our supporters.

Revolutionary Power

Revolutionary Power

AN ACTIVIST'S GUIDE TO THE ENERGY TRANSITION

Shalanda H. Baker

 **ISLAND**PRESS | Washington | Covelo

Library of Congress Control Number: 2020939056

All Island Press books are printed on environmentally responsible materials.

Manufactured in the United States of America
10 9 8 7 6 5 4 3 2 1

Keywords: American Legislative Exchange Council (ALEC), centralized energy system, climate fundamentalism, community energy, distributed energy, energy democracy, energy equity, energy insecurity, energy justice, energy poverty, environmental justice, green bank, Hawai'i energy generation, Hurricane Maria, investment tax credit (ITC), net energy metering (NEM), New York Climate Leadership and Community Protection Act (CLCPA), Public Utilities Regulatory Policies Act (PURPA), Puerto Rico energy generation, renewable portfolio standards

Contents

For Chuck and Connie

Introduction

I have to start at the beginning. I didn't set out to write a book about energy justice. My journey to write *Revolutionary Power: An Activist's Guide to the Energy Transition* is as improbable as my current role as a law professor. I grew up in Austin, Texas, a sprawling, liberal college town in the heart of a deep red state. My mother played the role of mom and dad and encouraged us to go to college, despite a lack of resources to finance a college education. I excelled in sports, made a name for myself as a student leader, and somehow found my way to the United States Air Force Academy for college.

I spent four years at the academy quietly aware of injustice and structural inequality. I was a Black, queer, young woman discovering her sexuality during the height of "Don't Ask, Don't Tell," a government policy that banned military service for LGBT people. I quickly learned to code shift and blend into the military's straight, largely white, male environment.

As a cadet and young officer, I got involved with the wrong partner. The intimate partner violence I experienced in that relationship made me realize the unique burdens placed on service members who take a vow to serve their country, but yet cannot live freely and openly because of whom they love. I eventually left the military under the shadow of "Don't Ask, Don't Tell" and committed the rest of my professional life to service in pursuit of social justice.

My experiences in the military and subsequent work in the nonprofit sector inspired me to go to law school. After graduation, I found myself, improbably, working at a large, corporate law firm as a project finance lawyer. I spent my days learning how to put together large energy project transactions, ranging from the dirtiest of energy sources to renewable energy. In practice, I became familiar with financing documents, environmental regulations, federal energy regulations, real estate, and, of course, the oil and gas industry.

In 2008, I received a transfer to the law firm's Tokyo office. It was an exciting and heady time for me. I landed in Tokyo one week after Lehman Brothers declared bankruptcy and found myself living and working in Japan during the largest global financial disaster since the Great Depression. In an emotional year filled with highs and lows, I witnessed the election of our country's first Black president, Barack Obama; my family struggled with unemployment and underemployment; and the US federal government rushed to bail out the very banks whose staggering risk-taking had led to the financial crisis. I also watched as my colleagues—senior partners at the law firm—worked to protect wealthy corporate clients from the disintegration of the global financial system. Meanwhile, symptoms of ecological collapse became increasingly apparent. In 2008, we collectively witnessed the hottest year on record, a milestone that we have successively plowed through nearly every year thereafter.[1] That year marked a turning point for me. I had decided to become a lawyer to make the world a better place, not to help perpetuate inequality and preserve a broken system. I saw the twin crises of the global financial crisis and climate change as symptoms of a much larger problem, and I wanted to be part of the solution.

In July 2009, I left the practice of law. I left legal practice with massive law school debt, but with enough savings to create a bridge to whatever was next. I had heard about Afro-Indigenous peoples in Colombia fighting against dirty coal mines, and I wanted to be part of that fight. I moved to Mexico to brush up on the Spanish I had learned as a girl living in bilingual, bicultural Austin and planned to work my way down to Bogotá, where I had spent part of a prior vacation making contacts. I never made it to Bogotá.

Instead, I spent the bulk of the next year living in southern Mexico in Oaxaca, a place known for its staggering physical beauty, high poverty rates, and rich Indigenous culture. In January 2010, I landed in the city of Oaxaca on a one-way ticket, with the only sure thing being that I would work with someone, somewhere, against injustice. While there, I worked with Indigenous weavers who were hoping to learn enough English to bargain on equal footing with the many tourists who came there seeking a deal on artisan rugs. As I lost myself in the mountains and ocean in Oaxaca, I shed some of the anxieties of my life as a corporate lawyer. Before I had left for Mexico, a mentor had convinced me to pursue my dream of teaching law, so I planted a few seeds for a future as an academic, unsure of whether they would take root.

Over the next few months, my teaching dreams took shape, and I accepted a position as a teaching fellow at the University of Wisconsin School of Law. Two weeks before my scheduled departure back to the United States, I came across a large festival in one of Oaxaca City's main parks. Indigenous activists had organized the festival to share stories about the impacts of genetically modified corn on heritage corn species; struggles for sovereignty over natural resources, such as water and land; and the fight against large-scale wind energy development in a place called the Isthmus of Tehuantepec.

I listened to all the stories with fascination and indignation, but when a group of Indigenous farmers and a teacher from the isthmus took the stage to speak about their struggles against corporate interests moving into the area to build large, utility-scale wind farms, an electric current moved through my spine. It's hard to explain, but I knew, in that moment, that this tension—between Indigenous rights and clean energy, between the rush to avert catastrophic climate change and social justice—would form the foundation of my work as an activist and scholar. It would also become my life's work.

I introduced myself to the speakers, and within days I found myself in Juchitán, Oaxaca, the small town at the epicenter of the extensive wind energy development taking place in the region. In Juchitán, I spoke with the same farmers and activists who had attended the meeting at the Oaxaca City park. They invited me to a meeting deep in the mountains of the isthmus, where dozens of Indigenous people had traveled to discuss *megaproyectos* (megaprojects) and the impacts of such development on their livelihoods. When those fighting against the wind development rose to speak, they told a story that mirrored the stories I had heard about mining in Afro-Indigenous communities in Colombia. Their struggles echoed the stories of countless communities around the world affected by oil and gas development: dispossession, displacement, environmental harm, unfair contracts, racism, and a litany of concerns about impacts to culture and community.

As I listened to the story of wind development in Oaxaca, I realized that we—the collective we—are poised to replicate the very injustices of the dirty energy industry in the name of *clean* energy or, much more insidiously, in the name of averting catastrophic climate change. As long as we use the same mechanisms of development—from the corporate models to the finance and development models—it seems that we, those with power to dictate the path of development, will sacrifice the most vulnerable people on the planet—poor people, Indigenous people—for "clean" energy. That day began my journey to write *Revolutionary Power*.

About This Book

This book reflects what I have learned on my journey, from that dusty meeting hall deep in the mountains of Oaxaca, Mexico, to Hawai'i, where, as a law professor, I quickly realized that in the United States we are not immune to replicating inequality in our efforts to combat climate change, to Puerto Rico, California, New York, and the many places in between. The experiences of those who live in these places form the heart of the story we are telling ourselves about the trade-offs required to transition from fossil fuels to clean, renewable energy.

Throughout this book. I spend a great deal of time discussing Hawai'i's energy transition. From 2014 to 2017, I had a front-row seat to the state's efforts to craft and implement laws and policies to transition its energy system from one dependent on fossil fuels to one completely dependent on renewable energy by 2045. In Hawai'i, I cut my energy policy teeth on the complex regulatory issues and sociocultural dimensions of that place. I also began to understand the dimensions of energy justice.

I recount much of that journey here because I see Hawai'i's transition as a model of what states, advocates, and other stakeholders should and should not do as they struggle to transition away from fossil fuels. As stakeholders involved in Hawai'i's renewable energy transition have noted, Hawai'i's energy system is a microcosm of the broader US energy system. The state has abundant renewable energy resources, as well as an aging electricity grid that is showing strain in its attempts to incorporate more intermittent renewable energy sources. Like the broader United States, Hawai'i is also a picture of extremes: extreme wealth and extreme economic hardship. The state's heavy reliance on fossil fuels also exposes it to the energy market's volatility and uncertainty, particularly given that those resources arrive in Hawai'i on ships. As an island state, Hawai'i arguably faces higher stakes in getting climate and energy policy right. It also seems uniquely positioned to do so. As many have observed, if that state gets its renewable energy transition right on a small scale, other states might be able to replicate aspects of its transition. If the state gets it wrong, however, what state *can* get it right? For these reasons, I spend much time dissecting the many dimensions of Hawai'i's transition. I also frequently draw on examples from other places that offer lessons regarding the country's transition away from fossil fuels.

I could not tell the stories within *Revolutionary Power* without sharing the context of my personal story and the unique path I have walked as a woman, a queer person, and a Black person. In this book, I share stories about my own life and the way the energy system has shaped my family's experiences and its trajectory. I have a stake in our global energy transition. My life experiences and the deepest roots of my family tree interweave to bias me against entrenched power and oppression. My experiences lead me always to question the efficacy of the current path. I need you to know this, dear reader, before you start this book.

Why This Book Right Now?

There are many reasons to write a book about climate change, the environment, and renewable energy right now. Global warming–induced climate change exposes the inequities within our global society. Climate change peels back the preexisting vulnerabilities that the poor, people of color, and Indigenous communities face as catastrophic floods, fires, and weather events become more frequent. As the Intergovernmental Panel on Climate Change warns, the climate changes ahead will undoubtedly disproportionately burden the poor, communities of color, island nations, and Indigenous peoples.[2] They are the first impacted and the worst impacted.[3] These communities tend to live on the most marginal land (such as low-lying, flood-prone areas and former toxic waste sites) within a community, and they also lack the economic resources needed to bounce back from climate change–related events. Advocates fear that climate change will not only expose the deep inequalities that exist around the world, but exacerbate them.

Many have taken the call, spiritual and otherwise, to sound urgent alarms about the future ahead of us. It is worth mentioning that the strongest and most well-publicized voices arguing for climate action have emanated from the dominant Western culture. With few exceptions, many of these voices—mainly White, mainly male—have alerted us to the dangers ahead, warning that even those with resources—namely, White, wealthy people—are not immune to climate disaster. This book takes a decidedly different tack. I argue that climate change positions those without power—namely Brown and Black people, low-income communities, and communities of color—to become both architects and beneficiaries of the new energy system.

I do not mean to critique the many important contributions to the climate movement, but I have written *Revolutionary Power* to arm those made vulnerable by the structure of the current energy system with what they need to remake that system in service of their humanity. I write for those at the margins, those whose lives have been intimately shaped by the past century of energy policy in the United States. I write for those so frequently shut out of decision-making that affects them, whose skin might be brown or black, and whose ancestors labored on plantations and in factories made prosperous by their cheap labor. I write to honor my own people, whose histories, hopes, and dreams are embedded upon the oil fields and bayous of Louisiana and Texas and whose blood courses through my veins. The unequal system of law and policy that required their existence and marginalization persists, but it now shows signs of buckling under the weight of the current climate emergency. I write to illustrate new possibilities for the energy system and to offer a radical reimagining of what might be possible for other aspects of our socioeconomic system when the energy system is just.

What Is This Book?

Revolutionary Power does not aim to develop or advance a particular theory, although it uses some theoretical and academic texts when needed to clarify or amplify a point. It is more like a book for the kitchen table, where friends gather to discuss the things that matter most in their lives. It is also, in part, my story, telling how I came to see energy policy and the energy system as the most important fronts in the battle to protect the civil rights of all people. It is also the story of all of us and the power of using the energy system to advance radical social change.

This book tells the story of this particular moment. We are living in the Anthropocene: a geologic era marked by humanity's devastating impact on Earth's atmosphere, waters, and soils. We did not collectively share in the creation of this devastation, and we will not share equally in its impacts. The Industrial Revolution that began in the 1880s in the western hemisphere created a model for development and a pattern of using Earth's resources that enrich the already powerful and imperil the most vulnerable.

In my work on this issue, I have learned that few really disagree with the following truth: climate change will force us to rethink the way we generate energy, distribute energy, and regulate the system. Our disagreements, however, lie in *how much* we will change the system. Will the system be redesigned to replicate the current structures of power and control, or will we reimagine our system to benefit those so often left out of discussions regarding system design?

This book provides the arrows in the quiver to everyone who wonders why the energy system, again and again, works against poor people, Indigenous people, and Brown and Black people. Rather than advance the range of equitable solutions to transform the transportation and building sectors, which form key and important portions of the broader energy system, this book focuses solely on the electricity sector and aspects of the energy system that feed into it. The poles, wires, and electricity generation facilities that power our homes, businesses, and sometimes vehicles make up the electricity sector. This book provides a step-by-step analysis of the key energy policy areas that are ripe for intervention within the electricity sector and, most importantly, arms readers with the rationale for *why* they should involve themselves in this particular fight.

My main objective is to model an approach of *justice first* in pursuit of averting catastrophic climate change rather than one of climate first, *justice later.* For many who feel the imminence of the climate disaster and who believe that the time to act on climate was last century, the idea of pursuing justice-oriented aims as we tackle climate change seems unwise, slow, and unwieldy. Their instinct is to focus first on shoring up the base and pick the lowest-hanging fruit and easy solutions to lower carbon emissions. I am not at odds with these people, but I would suggest that they look at the evidence.

In my experience, "easy" climate solutions might actually threaten to leave marginalized communities even more marginalized in the face climate change. I have seen how large-scale renewable energy projects displace and divide Indigenous communities and rural communities and have cumulative environmental impacts on ancestral land. I have also seen the very same corporate and financial interests that played a large role in developing and financing the fossil fuel–oriented projects that led to the current climate disaster jockey for space to maintain influence in the renewable energy economy, seeking to profit off the disaster they created.

In each of these examples, poor people, Indigenous peoples, and marginalized communities experience the same violence and economic exclusion in the clean energy economy that exists within the fossil fuel economy. I am not opposed to quick climate action, but I am against perpetuating injustice to save my own skin. I would ask, when we talk about low-hanging fruit, what do we mean? As a practical matter, it cannot mean putting unwavering trust in the very same entities and interests that got us into this disaster. As an ethical and moral matter, it cannot mean that we further burden and sacrifice those who were burdened and sacrificed under the prior system.

Put simply, solving the climate crisis cannot mean that we follow the same playbook of the past two hundred years. Solving the climate crisis requires that we turn the playbook on its head, introduce new players—those who were targeted as losers in the prior two centuries—and bring their concerns, hopes, and dreams to the forefront in the design of the new system. And in case there was any doubt, a new system is inevitable. The question is whether we will build that system on a foundation of justice and equity or whether we will build that system using the very same tools that landed us in this disaster in the first place. As a framework and approach to the new energy system, this book provides a path forward, a way rooted in concrete interventions, rationales, and strategies for a justice-centered transition away from fossil fuels.

Revolutionary Power makes three central claims. First, energy connects to every aspect of life, and the energy system defines nearly every aspect of socioeconomics and health. Second, the transition away from the fossil fuel–driven energy system offers an opportunity to upend existing socioeconomic inequality and foster lasting structural change. Although these first two claims are not altogether new, the book's third claim—and novel contribution—is to situate the technical domain of renewable energy policy within a broader civil rights discourse concerning inequality and access to justice.

Further, I argue that people of color, poor people, and Indigenous people must serve as the architects of the new system. They must actively engage in the creation of the new energy system so as to upend the embedded and unequal power dynamics that are a direct outgrowth of the current energy system. Rather than taking up arms to facilitate a revolution of the energy system, the revolution must be fought on the unfamiliar terrain of energy law and policy. This power revolution calls for the absolute transformation of fundamental aspects of the energy system: renewable energy policy, the financial institutions and quasi-financial institutions that fund energy projects, and the utility sector itself.

These claims go hand in hand with calls for a Green New Deal, which ties the urgency to avert catastrophic climate change to the need for comprehensive structural changes across all sectors of our economy, including the energy system. The Green New Deal's tent is large. It encompasses labor justice and access to jobs with dignity, economic justice and guarantees to a living wage, investments in public infrastructure, the guarantee of basic human rights, and the rebuilding of the social safety net. *Revolutionary Power* aligns with the broader principles of the Green New Deal and posits that this unique moment in history—when states across the country are transitioning a 100-year-old fossil fuel–based energy system to one based largely on renewable energy resources—provides an unprecedented opening for structural change. In the same ways that the Green New Deal's advocates seek to use decarbonization as gateway to a more fair and just society, *Revolutionary Power* provides an advocacy framework to transform the power relationships embedded within the electricity sector, a transformation that, I believe, will also lead to broader social change. This book is a playbook for the transformation.

Structure of This Book

Chapter 1, Energy, Energy Justice, and Civil Rights, contextualizes energy within the broader movement for civil rights. The chapter sketches out the broader linkages among movements for civil rights, Indigenous rights, economic justice, and health justice and argues that the structure of the energy system forms a central component of each movement's claims. It argues that although the fights for environmental justice in communities despoiled by the energy system, protests to prevent the building of more pipelines to carry fossil fuels across the United States, and access to ever-elusive economic prosperity are important battles, the true opportunities for system transformation lie in the current restructuring of the energy system, occurring across several policy domains.

Chapter 1 also makes the case for energy system transformation as a civil rights issue, building on the claims made by environmental justice activists and scholars since the early 1980s. The chapter synthesizes the environmental justice literature and illustrates that environmental justice issues—namely, the toxic by-products of the modern energy system—are also a legacy of racism. It also outlines the contours of energy justice and ends with the argument that climate change poses an existential threat to low-income communities and communities of color that creates an urgency to design an energy system rooted in equitable access to clean energy, economic justice, and restorative justice. Moreover, the chapter argues, the framework for building an equitable energy system already exists.

Chapters 2 through 6 provide rationales and strategies to engage in policy advocacy. Each chapter proceeds in three parts. Each begins with an overview of what is at stake in a particular policy and why it matters for marginalized communities. This overview grounds the reader in the true racial and economic justice stakes of the particular policy issue. The second section of each chapter examines and provides examples of what is wrong with the current approach to energy policy. Each chapter then ends with a discussion of concrete strategies to advance equity and justice.

Chapter 2, Utility Reform: The Linchpin to Transforming the Energy System, provides an overview of the structure of investor-owned utilities, including the ways the regulatory system provides perverse incentives to utilities that ultimately harm low-income communities and communities of color and prevent broader ownership of distributed energy generation projects. The chapter evaluates efforts to reform the utility sector, focusing primarily on Hawai'i and California, and concludes with an overview of the ways that utilities might be regulated or restructured to facilitate a just transition away from fossil fuels.

Chapter 3, Ending Climate Change Fundamentalism, turns to the ambitious state legislation meant to drive the renewable energy transition. The chapter defines climate change fundamentalism as the narrow focus on advancing climate and clean energy policy while failing to account for justice concerns or, more insidiously, deliberately delaying justice considerations. The chapter explores the equity dimensions of the current wave of ambitious clean energy policy enactments across the United States. The chapter starts broadly, pointing to the larger movement for the clean energy transition, and then argues that the current movement, primarily led by the so-called Big Green environmental organizations (for example, Sierra Club, Natural Resources Defense Council, Environmental Defense Fund, Greenpeace), currently lacks a coherent or consistent position concerning racial and economic justice. To make this claim, this chapter relies on empirical data gathered from California, a jurisdiction where racial and economic justice should form the centerpiece to any policy advancing a clean energy future. The chapter then illustrates how a climate change fundamentalism approach to the energy transition will likely lead to the replication of structural inequality. It concludes with concrete strategies to implement ambitious clean energy policies grounded in equity.

Chapters 4 and 5 examine the specific policies that states have adopted to meet ambitious clean energy goals. Chapter 4, The Fight for Local Power, addresses the energy justice dimensions of rooftop solar policies and provides an historical overview of one popular policy framework, net energy metering. As access to distributed renewable energy increased and became more available to low-income communities and communities of color, investor-owned utilities began an aggressive campaign to limit access, relying, ironically, on the argument that net energy metering and increased access to clean energy harm low-income communities and communities of color. This chapter provides examples from Hawaiʻi and Arizona, jurisdictions where the utilities effectively deployed such strategies. It ends with concrete approaches to net energy metering and successors to net energy metering rooted in equity.

Chapter 5, Community Energy: The Devil Is in the Details, examines and critiques common approaches to community energy. It argues that many community energy policies designed to offer low-income communities access to distributed energy generation fail to provide communities with opportunities for ownership and economic participation. The chapter illustrates how community energy projects may actually operate to reify inequality and benefit the wealthy rather than create wealth for low-income communities of color. Here I rely on data culled from Hawaiʻi's failed community energy efforts and conclude with an overview of ways to advance equitable community energy policy.

Chapter 6, Access to Capital: A Way to End Solar Segregation, addresses the financial aspects of the clean energy transition, including the ways marginalized communities are structurally excluded from accessing financial tools to advance local clean energy development. This chapter explores the "green banks" and "green funds" that states have developed to help facilitate the clean energy transition but that have not led to wealth creation in low-income communities of color. The Connecticut Green Bank, New York's Green Bank, and the Hawaiʻi's Green Energy Market Securitization financing program provide factual context for the discussion. The chapter concludes with a set of recommendations to shape green financial innovations consistent with energy justice.

The final chapter, Revolutionary Power, provides a call to action. Here I return to the civil rights framing and argue for a radical, structural transformation of the energy system rooted in racial and economic justice. This chapter reviews the key policy points raised throughout the book and argues for urgent action by all people—but namely people of color, Indigenous peoples, low-income communities, and those who have been harmed by the current energy system—to participate in the construction of a new energy system consistent with the principles of energy justice.

A Word on the Politics of Climate Change

Before we begin this journey together, allow me to try to head off any critiques that this book is anticlimate or antiprogress or that I would rather see stagnation on climate action than true climate progress that makes "compromises" on issues of justice and equity. I am deeply aligned with the goals of the climate movement, but I cannot align myself with a movement that in any way willingly compromises the existence, prosperity, or future prospects of any people. I cannot align with a movement, scholars, or policy makers who ignore the ill effects of the existing energy system and who have no commitments to designing a new system that remedies these harms.

Even before writing this book, and since the beginning of my academic career, I have heard pushback from academics and policy makers regarding whether centering equity in the fight against climate change is realistic given the short time line that remains to act on climate. Let me be clear: climate change will define our very existence on this planet for decades—no, centuries—to come. Mainstream climate change advocates have advanced a narrative that we lack the time to integrate justice and equity concerns into law and policy efforts to avert catastrophic climate change. I strongly disagree. Buying into a discourse that centers the primacy of *action* over the primacy of *people* is inherently unsustainable and will inevitably lead to even greater instability than climate change portends. We can ill afford, at this time of such vast and devastating inequality, to take a conscious gamble on energy policies that virtually guarantee that those harmed by the old energy system will suffer continued harm, or worse. Moreover, the type of energy opportunities our policies seek to expand—renewable energy—lends itself to greater economic and social participation than the dirty energy resources of the past. Renewable energy offers a once-in-a-century chance to reshape our relationship to the energy system and advance greater equity.

We need now, more than ever, revolutionary power, an approach to our energy system that centers the voices, hopes, and dreams of the poor, people of color, Indigenous people, and those marginalized by the old energy system in the redesign of the new system. This book provides a step-by-step guide to achieve this goal. It won't be easy, but the common critiques—that this approach is too hard, too slow, or too unrealistic—will eventually give way to the inevitable truth: revolutionary power is the only pathway out of this climate crisis. May this book—part autobiography, part policy guide, and (daringly) part love story for the planet—form a crucial part of our journey.

CHAPTER 1

Energy, Energy Justice, and Civil Rights

Lineage is a funny thing when you are Black in America. On my father's side, our branches of the family tree end abruptly in nubby points, their leaves lost somewhere on the path between Lake Charles, Louisiana, and Port Arthur, Texas. Dad grew up in the Carver Terrace housing projects of Port Arthur, Texas, a low-income, mostly Black and Latinx community about an hour and a half away from Houston. It sits on the Gulf Coast, the skyline defined by the blinking lights of offshore oil rigs, petrochemical plants, a waste incinerator, and oil refineries.

I visited Port Arthur for the first time when I was eight. Prince's "When Doves Cry" was all over the radio. I remember my first day in town, my dad driving me and my sister around, blaring Prince, and then pulling into a long row of cars parked up against the coastline. It was not pretty. The sulfuric air stung my nostrils, uninitiated as I was to the smell of a refinery town. The brownish water did not look like the blue-green sea from the books I read. It was a murky brown. It carried a stench, but my dad and the other men dipped their nets and lines, in search of shrimp, crab, and fish, into the oil-slicked waters. That night, relatives from around town and the neighboring town of Beaumont gathered at my dad's house for a fish fry: fried fish filled with tiny bones, Gulf shrimp that melted in your mouth, hush puppies tightly bound up with spices, and tangy coleslaw mixed with a healthy amount of mayonnaise. We ate other foods I had never heard of, too: boudain, a spicy blood sausage filled with pork and rice; fried oysters; and crawfish you broke open with your teeth, their insides invading your mouth with briny water.

Port Arthur captivated my sister and me. We fell in love that summer. My dad had a good job working for the local energy company, Entergy. On his days off, he lounged inside, but gave me and my sister a dollar each (a veritable jackpot) to fill our bellies with candy from the local gas station (me: always Snickers and Dr. Pepper; my sister: always something sour and Sprite). Dad had an incredible sense of humor. His entire body shook with his retelling of "How I met yo' mama" and of the time I climbed a tree when I could barely walk and they only found me after hearing my muted moans from the tree's highest branches. The stories and accents were a patchwork of a life both foreign and familiar to me. Many say that folks in that part of Texas have more in common with their neighbors in Louisiana than Texans, from the hot sauce to the Cajun and Creole bloodlines that run along Highway 10, connecting bayous, cypress groves, and swamps to communities filled with people living close to the land. I looked like my father, his brothers, my cousins. We shared a genealogy, but hundreds of miles separated our lives and trajectories.

Our grandfather had deep black skin, the kind of color they call "blue-black." We spent some days at his house, a shotgun house with various rooms still unfinished, but filled with plenty of curiosities to occupy our young minds. We learned to play jacks on the weathered linoleum kitchen floor, which buckled in certain spots to reveal dirt-caked wood planks underneath. From our grandfather's house, we had our routes. The first stop was across the tracks to the Hostess "bakery."

Everything on discount. Heaven for me. That summer, we filled up on Twinkies, Ding Dongs, and Honey Buns, all available for the coins our dad's job provided us. Grandpa lived on the east side of town with his second wife, my uncles, and my aunt. They owned a juke joint and pool hall up the road on Houston Avenue, so after the bakery stop, we walked up the road away from Grandpa's house and the bakery a piece. Lunch at the pool hall was fried chicken pressed between two pieces of Rainbow brand white bread. From there, we'd retrace our steps, sometimes gobbling up homemade Kool-Aid ice pops from a neighbor (ten cents!) while en route. We journeyed up the road, passing a neighborhood filled with mostly well-kept modest houses behind chain-link fences and passing the scary houses overrun with weeds, back to Grandpa's, back to playing jacks and running through the shotgun house.

I adored my Uncle D, a playful teenager, all "Baker" in his facial features (full cheeks marked by deep dimples, dancing eyes), sense of humor, and sharp wit. I frequently goaded my uncle into wrestling matches. One time, my skinny leg slid under the couch, catching against a rusty nail poking down through the couch's fabric. I lay on the couch as my uncle slowly poured an entire bottle of hydrogen peroxide over my leg, the exposed white tissue oozing and bubbling as I writhed around in pain. Uncle D wanted to be a doctor, I was told, so there would be no trip to the emergency room to stitch the gash that ran about an inch horizontally on my skinny thigh. Instead, he patched me up and cleaned the wound with a care I'll never forget.

The Energy System as Destiny

I didn't realize it then, but my dad's family was poor. They lived in what I now know is a classic environmental justice community shaped almost entirely by the oil industry.[1] Poor people and people of color are more likely than others to live in the shadows of major energy facilities or in communities that house waste generated by power plants.[2] The children who grow up in such frontline or environmental justice communities face an array of toxic exposures that shape their lives.

A decade after the passage of extensive environmental legislation that served as the high-water mark for the mainstream environmental movement, the concerns of frontline communities took center stage. In 1983, protesters in Warren County, North Carolina, clashed with authorities over the dumping of toxic waste in a poor, majority Black community. The protests, which resulted in hundreds of arrests and galvanized civil rights leaders in support of an environmental cause, launched the environmental justice movement.[3] Four years later, in 1987, the United Church of Christ published the landmark report "Toxic Wastes and Race," which established the strong link between race and environmental burden.[4] It came at a time when scholars like Robert Bullard were beginning to sound alarms over "environmental racism," a term that refers to "any environmental policy, practice or directive that differentially affects or disadvantages (whether intended or unintended) individuals, groups or communities based on race or color."[5] Our political, economic, governmental, legal, and military institutions effectively sanction environmental racism through "public policies and industry practices [that] provide *benefits* for whites while shifting *costs* to people of color."[6]

Since then, academics and advocates have devoted their entire careers to remedying the environmental harms that disproportionately impact communities of color and ensuring that the concerns of impacted communities make their way into environmental policies. Advocates saw President Bill Clinton's 1994 issuance of Executive Order 12898, Federal Actions to Address Environmental Justice in Minority Populations and Low-Income Populations, as a victory. The order links directly to the Civil Rights Act of 1964, which prohibits discrimination among agencies receiving federal funds.[7] It also directs federal agencies to "improve methodologies for assessing and mitigating impacts, health effects from multiple and cumulative exposure, collection of data on low-income and minority populations who may be disproportionately at risk, and impacts on subsistence fishers and consumers of wild game" and to increase participation of frontline communities in the environmental impact assessment process.[8] Yet years later, environmental harms, allocated by race and income, persist.[9] True gains have been slow to materialize.

Port Arthur is small, at around 55,000 people. Certain census tracts are more than 77 percent African American, and others are 30 to 65 percent Latinx.[10] The median Hispanic and African American household incomes are $33,000 and $25,300, respectively, which means that it is a tough place to prosper, let alone survive.[11] About 15 percent of the residents are unemployed,[12] and 30 percent of the residents live under the poverty line, making it one of the poorest communities in the state.[13] And yet, Port Arthur, and its nearby neighbors, Beaumont and Orange, form what is known as the Golden Triangle. The gold refers either to the vast amount of wealth extracted from the soil by the region's extraordinary number of refineries or to the blinking lights that appear on nighttime satellite images of the region, identifying the refineries and petrochemical plants that define this triangular expanse of southeast Texas.

In 1901, oil prospectors struck oil with a 1,000-foot-deep well dug into Spindletop Hill just outside of Beaumont. At 150 feet high, the geyser was the most powerful ever seen in the world at that time. The modern oil industry—including Texaco, Exxon, and Gulf Oil—can trace its origins to that single oil strike. It is not an overstatement to claim that the Spindletop strike changed the oil and gas industry forever. In fact, a monument to the strike notes that the well "ushered in a 'new era in civilization.'"[14] Despite the untold fortunes made in the Golden Triangle, the environmental, social, and health burdens evident in communities throughout region bring a startling clarity to the unjust trade-offs inherent in the design of the nation's energy system.

Three years before my first and only summer in Port Arthur, *Texas Monthly* named this oil-rich piece of Earth the Cancer Belt.[15] At the time of the article's publication, the cancer rate in Jefferson County, of which Port Arthur is a part, was 187 per 100,000 people, compared with 158.6 per 100,000 people in Texas and 174 per 100,000 people nationally. Lung cancer rates in the county were also high: 62.1 per 100,000 people, compared with the national rate of 42 per 100,000 people. Cancer stalked entire communities and seemed linked to the scores of petrochemical factories dotting the region, as well as the poor air quality in the area. By one account, the communities around the "Golden Triangle exuded stenches that were described as smelling like anything from burning cabbage to burning skunk."[16] Many believed that the plants were making them sick, but they feared biting the hand that fed their communities.

Over time, environmental conditions in the area have worsened. The US Environmental Protection Agency ranks Port Arthur as among the worst in the country for toxic chemical emissions, and according to one article, "virtually everyone in the city is affected by serious health problems. Deaths from cancer, even among young people, surprise no one."[17] Cancer rates in the county remain high, but among Black residents, they are devastating. According to a 2017 NAACP report, "the cancer mortality rate for Black county residents was nearly 40 percent higher than the state average."[18] On the whole, county residents face an "added cancer risk from hazardous air pollutants . . . at a rate of 670 parts per million, compared to the overall rate in the state of Texas of 550 parts per million. Even more startling, the 'added cancer risk in Jefferson County is also 670 times higher than the goal of the Clean Air Act.'"[19] A 2001 study found that more than 80 percent of the residents on the mostly Black west side of Port Arthur suffered in some way from heart and lung problems.[20] Studies have linked such exposures to heart disease and other cardiopulmonary ailments.[21] According to Goldman Prize winner and environmental activist Hilton Kelley, "One in five West Port Arthur households has someone in it with respiratory illness."[22]

Although "thousands of chemical facilities" dot the entire Gulf Coast region and the region is home to four of the ten largest US oil and gas refineries,[23] Port Arthur alone shoulders the environmental burden of the five-and-a-half-square-mile Motiva refinery (the nation's largest), as well as five more petrochemical plants, the Veolia incinerator facility, and the terminus for the controversial Keystone XL tar sands pipeline.[24] Until it was demolished in 2015, the Carver Terrace housing project where my father spent part of his childhood butted right up against the Valero (formerly Gulf Oil) and Motiva (formerly Texaco) refineries, separated only by a fence.[25] Long before "shelter in place" entered into the broader lexicon due to the global coronavirus outbreak of 2020, residents in the Golden Triangle learned to heed the chilling warnings from officials telling them to cover their windows with plastic tarps and tape and to avoid going outside so as to prevent breathing in toxic air.[26]

My family comes from this place. Sometimes a song, the smell of frying fish, or salt hitting the warm air a certain way takes me back to that first and only summer I spent in Port Arthur. Uncle D never became a doctor. Like Grandpa and my dad, and my younger half-brother, he worked in the energy industry. About twenty years after the summer he nursed my leg back to health, a falling object at a refinery hit him in the head. He was never the same, but he retired early with disability benefits.[27]

My father cut an imposing figure in any setting. At six feet five inches tall, he was a star football player, star basketball player, and star track athlete. According to his only surviving brother, my dad remains the most well-known wide receiver at the local Black high school, Lincoln

High, from which he graduated more than fifty years ago. He and his brothers were the "Baker boys," legendary athletes and an inseparable troupe. Dad was an All-American and earned a full scholarship to the nationally ranked and storied football program at the University of Nebraska, but as he told me, he left after one year on campus because it was just "too White." He left Nebraska for Texas Southern University, a historically Black college where he met my mother, a middle-class Catholic schoolgirl from the multiracial mecca of San Antonio. They spent a glorious year strutting and peacocking together on that campus until my mom got pregnant, they dropped out, and they both joined the service—he, army; and she, the civil service.

I came along in 1976, right before my mom's twenty-first birthday and while my sister was still in diapers. We all left for Germany, where my parents got stationed. Family lore has it that my mom and dad had a side hustle. They'd invited folks over to party, and, for a fee, the party-goers could partake in the hashish on hand at the party. My mother, the queen of the side hustle, realized that my dad was enjoying the party a little bit too much and that he was, effectively, smoking up their profits. They split up. My mom bounced around, going from Germany to California to San Antonio and, eventually, to Austin. She raised us in Austin with limited support from my father and begrudging support from my maternal grandmother, who never forgave her daughter for dropping out of college and marrying my dad, a charismatic athlete from, in her words, "the ghetto."

Port Arthur, its refineries, and its poverty shaped my dad's life after us. Like his dad, who worked at the large Texaco (now Motiva) factory abutting the Carver Terrace housing projects, my father got a job in the energy business, working at the generating plant for the fossil fuel–driven local utility, Entergy. The job does not sound very sexy on paper, but for him it offered something close to a middle-class life. Despite the solid pay, I can only imagine what he, a former high school standout athlete with sharp wit and big dreams, must have felt each day he went to work at the plant spewing toxic fumes into his community. I often wonder what happened to his hopes and dreams. He got hooked on crack. The first and only summer my sister and I spent in Port Arthur, I watched as my dad and his girlfriend peeled twenty-dollar bills off of impossibly thick rolls of cash, made stops here and there to pick up "stuff," and implored me and my sister to go outside and play.

By his forties, my dad had type 2 diabetes and the beginning of heart disease, ailments no doubt linked to a lifetime spent in Port Arthur's toxic haze. Around that time, he was at the plant just outside of town, and he didn't feel right. He asked his boss if he could leave the plant to go to his doctor. His boss refused, but my dad, sensing that something was wrong with his body, left anyway. When he got to the doctor's office, the doctor said that if my father had arrived just a couple of minutes later, he would have died. Armed with that news, my dad called the plant. Within days, he had an early retirement package in his hands.

My dad died a few years later, at fifty-three. Too young. The cause of death was heart disease, the same disease that took his older brother's life (who died at thirty-eight). I never got to ask him about his mother, Mary Helen, a fierce, beautiful woman who raised him and his two brothers in the housing projects. I never got to know her because she also died too young, at forty-four years old, of cancer and heart disease. I never got to ask him why he turned to crack and how he eventually freed himself of its grip. I never asked him what it felt like to know how incredibly talented he was, physically and intellectually, but to be confined and limited by a place. It wasn't until many years later, when I saw the whole of his community as an environmental justice community and the birthplace of the modern petroleum industry, that these questions danced around my brain, finding their way into my life's work.[28]

My dad's story, my family's story, and heck, our *national* story, are all bound up in Port Arthur, a place where race intersects with policy choices around energy and the environment and where an industry gives—through the prospect of wealth and stability—and takes away—through workplace injuries, public health crises, commodification of Brown and Black bodies, and so much environmental devastation. It is a true sacrifice zone. The lives and future prospects of Black and Brown people are sacrificed to support the nucleus of the modern energy industry.

I didn't realize how much my father's story would stay with me, how it would form the undercurrent of my work, even as I worked as a corporate energy lawyer, moved to Japan, and later moved to Mexico and Hawai'i. Once again, I have scrambled to the top of the tree. This time I am perched among the highest branches of my own family's tree, trying to understand the lives shaped by an industry and to discern how their stories contribute to the corpus of a US energy story filled with injustice and with lives cut way too short by structural inequality.

Our people—scattered in communities along the road that stretches from Port Arthur, Texas, to Lake Charles, Louisiana—were the enslaved and colonized. Perhaps it is no mistake then that the energy system born out of that same soil produces so much wealth in the United States and simultaneously makes life nearly unbearable for Black and Brown bodies.[29] The energy system has, in many ways, swapped out one system of extraction—legalized slavery—and replaced it with a more modern one, where oppression does not live in the lash, but in the toxic molecules that pollute our communities in higher numbers, wedge into our airways and waterways, and kill us.

The modern energy system is destiny. It defines communities quite literally, with fence lines demarcating livable space and the refinery, and structurally, with economic opportunities that come at great environmental costs and health risks. Although much about the energy system seems fixed, at this particular moment in our collective history, climate change and technological advances provide an unprecedented window to reshape our energy system to advantage those who are the most burdened within it. The energy transition provides an opening to change destiny. Given the profound ways the system interacts with poor people, low- to moderate-income people, and people of color, this imperative—to remake the energy system in the image of equity and justice—is no different than the freedom struggles of the mid-twentieth century. The struggle for energy justice, for revolutionary power, is about nothing less than freedom.

The Energy System as Power

The energy system reflects power. Yes, the system literally provides power, but the system itself represents the sum total of a series of political and economic choices that concentrate power and wealth in the hands of utility companies and their investors, often at the expense of utility customers. Climate change and the stronger storms, fires, and floods that it brings with it expose the underlying inequities that have shaped communities and highlight the need for local energy sources that are owned and controlled by communities. Climate change also exposes the inherent political and economic power embedded within the energy system. Although storms and power outages affect everyone, the most economically distressed among our communities have the most trouble bouncing back. These individuals live paycheck to paycheck, are disproportionately Brown and Black, and often have underlying health conditions that require reliance on life-saving home medical devices powered by electricity.

Today, as I write this book, one of the largest investor-owned utilities (IOUs) in the United States, Pacific Gas and Electric (PG&E), has elected to cut power to hundreds of thousands of residents in California, the world's fifth largest economy. All three of California's IOUs enacted the euphemistically named "Public Safety Power Shutoffs," but five of the ten most destructive fires in the state since 2015 have been connected to PG&E's system of delivering energy to residents.[30] The planned outages do not discriminate based on race or class, but they disproportionately impact the poorest residents, who can ill afford to replace refrigerators full of groceries and medicines. These residents also lack the ability to adapt easily to major weather events because, more often than not, they cannot afford expensive adaptive technologies like solar panels and battery storage that can offer a measure of backup power after storms, fires, and floods. By PG&E's admission, the utility's own equipment likely led to California's deadliest fire, the Camp Fire, in 2018, but the company elected to forgo repairing or replacing the equipment in order to save money, a choice consistent with the utility's history of putting profits over safety.[31]

To be clear, the state's utilities enacted the power shutoffs to prevent harm to residents due to wildfires sparked by the company's own equipment. PG&E, which in 2020 pleaded guilty to involuntary manslaughter,[32] has routinely been identified as a uniquely bad actor in California. The utility failed adequately to maintain its electric equipment, even by its own standards. Rather than replacing equipment that had outlived its useful life, the utility routinely ran its equipment to failure, an economic decision that lined the pockets of the utility's investors but had deadly consequences for many California families.[33]

California's experiences illustrate the link between the energy system's design and the lived experiences of those within it, but they are not an anomaly. In September 2017, for example, Hurricane Maria devastated the archipelago of Puerto Rico. This category 5 hurricane's destructive path started in the southeastern corner of the main island, cut a forty-five-degree angle through the center, and exited the island's northwest corner. Maria uprooted trees, stripped hillsides bare, and destroyed the power grid. The storm contributed to the deaths of more than four thousand people.[34] Without electricity, hundreds lacked the medical assistance needed to power oxygen tanks and dialysis machines. Puerto Ricans struggled to access the basics: food, water, shelter. Those who could not afford to flee the territory faced months without power; those in remote, mountainous regions and on the islands of Vieques and Culebra lived without electricity for more than a year. The centralized system of energy production exacerbated the critical lack of access to power in Puerto Rico, contributing to the high death tolls.

The same year that Hurricane Maria struck, Hurricane Harvey dumped more than fifty inches of rain in the Houston metropolitan area and threatened the spine of the nation's energy sector, located in the Houston and Port Arthur regions. Rather than rethinking the concentration of refineries and petrochemical facilities that burden the region, commentators and politicians sought to make the region more resilient to weather events. This decision, too, threatened to cement in place the many unequal health and environmental burdens borne by Port Arthur and other communities in the Golden Triangle. It is a choice that reflects the power and politics embedded in the system.

In 2012, Superstorm Sandy brought a storm surge so fierce that it devastated the nation's financial sector and left millions without power within the populous Northeast.[35] That same storm forced residents in high-rise buildings to cope with a lack of running water and access to vital energy to flush toilets, as well as keep medicines and foods cold. Similarly, disaster struck New Orleans and the surrounding area after Hurricane Katrina sent hundreds of poor people, mainly Black poor people, to their rooftops in 2005, waving white flags made of ripped T-shirts and sheets, to signal for help. Those who remained in New Orleans after the storm faced weeks (sometimes months) without electricity.[36] More recently have been the scores of tornadoes and floods that devastated poor, rural communities around the United States in 2019 alone, stripping households of earnings and life savings during planting and growing seasons.

In each of the foregoing cases, the choices made concerning the structure of the energy system directly affected the lives of the most vulnerable. When asked to consider the voices of low-income communities and the most vulnerable in energy policy decisions, however, those shaping the new energy system into one driven by clean, renewable resources treat energy as a purely technical issue, one in which the primary concern is only whether or not the lights go on. I have spoken and met with scores of energy policy wonks, and many illustrate an unwillingness to consider the social dimensions of the energy system. From the perspective of decision makers creating our new energy system, energy policy traverses the complex domain of technology and finance; it does not involve the social, the political, or the physical. It does not involve power.

Instead, the technological and financial feasibility of bringing more clean energy onto the grid becomes the focus of most policy debates. This overemphasis on technology and finance ignores the significant ways our energy system, created through a series of policy choices, shapes every single aspect of life, particularly for poor people and people of color. The human implications of the most technical aspects of energy policy rarely get discussed, and if they do, they are discussed as an after-the-fact consideration once the central features of the policy have been designed.

This perspective is evolving through the work of grassroots advocacy groups. The energy democracy movement sees this moment of transitioning away from fossil fuels as a unique opportunity to reimagine the energy system into one where power is literally and figuratively redistributed. In the energy democracy framing, communities and individuals, rather than large corporate entities and utilities, own and control the energy system and share in its economic benefits. Energy justice, also referred to as energy equity, strikes broader themes. Scholars of energy justice point to four common components: (1) distributive justice, which is the equitable allocation of benefits and burdens; (2) procedural justice, which means fair access to process; (3) recognition justice, which is acknowledgment of and respect for all peoples; and (4) restorative justice, which addresses issues of past harms.[37] In my work on energy justice, I have come to include an additional element: the centering of the voices of marginalized communities. The policy conversation begins with the concerns of those on the front lines of environmental degradation and climate change. Efforts should focus on how to reduce the multitude of burdens these communities face and provide for their social and economic inclusion in clean energy policy.

Under an energy justice approach to energy policy, each policy decision would be filtered through the lens of equity, which is to say that policy makers and other energy stakeholders would take into consideration past harms and burdens of the energy system when designing the new system. The creation of the policy would also involve those most impacted by it. Further, the policy would recognize the unique qualities of a community, account for past harms, and also center the voices of those most marginalized by the current energy system. Each framing—energy democracy and energy justice—elevates the concerns, hopes, and dreams of those historically marginalized by the energy system. The approaches create an extraordinary range of possibilities for the energy future.

Broadening access to local power and its local benefits to those most burdened under the current system requires the structural transformation of the energy system as we know it—and energy governance as we know it. It requires exposing the features of the energy system that disproportionately allocate power to those who are already wealthy and lifting up the concerns of those who have, for more than a century, been sacrificed in the name of the energy system. Energy justice and energy democracy provide the tools to recalibrate the power relationships embedded in the current system to ensure that our new clean energy system makes the concerns of the vulnerable a central feature of policy design.

The Energy System as Control

The centralized ownership, generation, and distribution of electricity resources by IOUs (such as PG&E) decrease competition and remove individuals from a position to dictate where and how they receive their energy. For many years, utilities were in the best position to make choices for electricity consumers; they had access to financial resources to build energy infrastructure and an incredible deal with the government that stated that, as long they supplied reliable electricity to customers, they would receive a reasonable return on the investments made in energy infrastructure. This deal, called the regulatory compact, incentivized utilities to invest in new electricity infrastructure, knowing that with every investment, the government guaranteed a reasonable rate of return. Much of this infrastructure included energy generation facilities, high-voltage transmission lines carrying electricity from generation facilities, electricity substations, and distribution lines to carry electricity from substations into homes. In most cases, the utility owned, operated, and controlled all these energy assets.

Today, the centralized model for owning and managing electricity resources makes less sense. New technology, such as solar panels and batteries, make individual ownership, control, and generation of electricity resources more of a possibility for low- to moderate-income people. The technology also offers an opportunity for individuals to access electricity even when natural disasters strike. In Puerto Rico, for example, those with solar panels recovered more quickly from the hurricane than their non-solar-powered neighbors; in California, those with solar panels and storage capacity worry less about the ongoing power outages orchestrated by the utilities. This decentralized power need not be an anomaly;

rather, it can be the blueprint for the future. Powerful stakeholders in favor of maintaining the current, centralized system have been hard at work to undermine a more decentralized power system and have begun a systematic assault on rooftop solar programs that hold promise for local control of electricity assets.

The energy system as it is currently constructed exerts an extraordinary amount of control over individual households and communities. Doubling down on the old, centralized model of energy ownership and distribution yields tangible, often negative, consequences. The energy system can dictate whether a person will have access to a life-saving medical device after a storm or will face a life-threatening medical disaster. It can dictate whether a household breathes in toxic fumes, whether the household owns its own clean energy system and has access to backup power due to an extreme weather event, and whether the household participates in a community-owned energy project that offers economic benefits at the household level. For these reasons, the design of the energy system matters. Too often, however, those who have the most to lose due to a lack of access to energy are the farthest from the policy-making table.

A Just Energy System as a Civil Right

We must view the battle for the design of the new, clean energy system through the same lens we use to view broader struggles for economic and civil rights. As environmental justice advocates have shown, the environmental racism faced in communities like Port Arthur leads directly to poor health outcomes, and we see similar patterns repeating themselves in the clean energy economy. Our work today, in this moment of transformation of our energy system to one built on cleaner energy, is to reveal the links between the design of the energy system, as effectuated through a series of energy policy decisions, and nearly every aspect of life.

The energy system routinely sacrifices Brown, Black, and Indigenous bodies to keep the lights on for the majority. Racial capitalism, as legal scholar Nancy Leong describes, is "the process of deriving social and economic value from the racial identity of another person."[38] In many ways, racial capitalism forms the bedrock of the global, fossil fuel–based energy system. In its current design, the energy system requires a permanent underclass that can be exploited and from which resources can be extracted. We see this clearly in Port Arthur, but we can also observe this phenomenon around the United States and throughout the global economy. Pipelines and transmission lines cut through rural communities and Indigenous lands, rendering valuable natural resources useless and compromised. This marginalization links to the nation's genocide of Indigenous peoples in the name of economic growth and American progress. The coal industry's barbaric practice of blasting the tops off mountains has also left deep scars on poor, White communities, also in furtherance of economic progress.

Transmuting these sacrificed landscapes and bodies into places that thrive requires that we understand the energy system's design. Physically, the fossil fuel economy requires a substantial, toxic footprint. Because fossil fuels are not located uniformly throughout our geography, certain communities, like Port Arthur, become sacrifice zones that are more prone to the array of health and environmental hazards detailed earlier in this chapter. This footprint explains why entire communities find themselves in harm's way. As environmental justice advocates have long highlighted, racism explains why people of color are more likely to live in such impacted communities, but rural communities and poor White people also suffer mightily within the current energy system. These White communities should tie their fates to those fighting for energy justice in Black and Brown communities.

Corporate entities and their close relative, IOUs—each driven by profit—also form the backbone of the energy system. The modern energy system depends on the investments of large corporate entities to extract, transport, refine, and burn the fossil fuels abundant in communities like those found in the Golden Triangle and coal country. As residents of Port Arthur know well, these corporate entities bristle against safety and health standards and are loathe to follow even the minimum federal standards regarding clean air. The fundamental misalignment between the entities relied on to shepherd energy resources from point to point and the broader public interest contributes to an unjust energy system.

This misalignment is replicated in the electricity sector. Since the early 1900s, we have relied on large IOUs to build the infrastructure needed to electrify our communities. As described in greater detail in chapter 2, IOUs operate much like the modern corporation, which can sometimes lead to the prioritization of shareholder profit over customer safety. The utilities' interest in keeping costs down can also lead to investments in large-scale clean energy developments that mirror the large-scale developments of the fossil fuel system, even when smaller-scale clean energy projects could reduce the environmental and social impacts of a larger project. These choices, along with the policies that permit them, further entrench inequality and racialized harm. In addition, IOUs have deep investments in, and commitments to, a sprawling system of poles and wires that, with the volatility of the climate change, may have outlived their usefulness. Unfortunately, IOUs have been slow to adjust to the new normal, putting all utility customers at risk and exposing the most vulnerable customers to life or death situations.

As the clean energy system begins to take shape around the world, we have a chance to remedy the harmful features of the fossil fuel system. The ubiquity of clean energy resources and innovations in the scale of clean energy production hold great promise for structural change, but we can already observe the emergence of new sacrifice zones in the name of clean energy, as well as a new form of racialized capital. For example, the state of Oaxaca in southern Mexico is the second poorest state in Mexico and home to no fewer than fourteen distinct Indigenous groups that speak distinct Indigenous languages. In the early 2000s, the US Department of Energy identified the Isthmus of Tehuantepec, the narrow strip of land sandwiched between the Atlantic and Pacific, as one of the windiest places in the world. Indigenous farmers and fishers live off of the land and ocean in the isthmus, the poorest place in Oaxaca state. The communities in the region have recently seen the exponential growth of wind farms in the area without the people's consultation or consent. The extraordinary amount of clean energy development in the region has done little to change the economic circumstances of the people in the isthmus, let alone offered a pathway to access cheap energy. Instead, the development has led to extensive conflict, dispossession, and environmental harm.[39] We are ready to turn the page of this familiar playbook, written and implemented by the fossil fuel industry all over the world, but we need a radically different text.

States around the United States have embarked on aggressive and ambitious campaigns to turn away from fossil fuels toward clean energy, but the very same mechanisms of racial and economic oppression that define the old system have already found their way into the new system design.[40] The stakeholders in charge of creating the new system fail to see or understand the intimate relationship that communities of color and low-income communities have with our energy system, and this failure has led them to bake the structural inequalities of the old system—power disproportionately held by IOUs and the corporations that generate energy, high costs, and sacrifice zones—into the policy design of the new system.

Each aspect of the energy system is up for grabs in the transition: the determination of who owns our energy resources and can access economic benefits attached to them; the fight for who can generate energy for their own use or their community's use; and the battle over how energy is distributed, at the local or regional level. The ability to access and shape energy policies that create clean air, clean water, open space, and affordable electricity turns on the design of the new system. Just as early environmental justice advocates drew the link between toxic dumping in Black communities and civil rights, the rights to access and shape clean energy policy in service of marginalized communities should be seen as part of the corpus of civil rights. Energy policy is the domain of the next generation of civil rights.

The Energy System as a Pathway to Revolution

Energy justice requires a reckoning with the impacts of the design of the energy system. It requires that those who, for too long, have borne the brunt of the centralized, fossil fuel–driven system move to the front of the line to receive the benefits of the new system. Energy justice requires that equity be a central part of energy policy. It requires a constant calibration of social, economic, and environmental harms through the policy-making lens. We are at a crossroads: our old, centralized energy system is already buckling under the weight of climate disasters threatening to render the most vulnerable among us even more vulnerable without access to vital power. A new future, one in which individuals own their own power systems and receive the economic benefits from them, is within reach as long as the levers for designing this system are made available to those who need them. As we move into this new future, we must also remember that a just transformation of our energy system requires a careful interrogation of the racist, capitalist politics that currently drive it. We must expose, and then eradicate, these underpinnings. True justice requires that the new design be based on an anti-racist, antioppression foundation.

No single aspect of the energy system, writ large, has been designed to benefit poor people, people of color, or Indigenous communities.

Over time, quite the opposite has been proven true. It therefore follows that, without a fight, even the policy mechanisms designed to avert catastrophic climate change will undoubtedly operate to harm our communities. Or, if the policies are not designed to be outright harmful, their benefits will be structurally inaccessible due to our society's ongoing marginalization and oppression of low-income communities and communities of color. Now is the time for extreme vigilance and activism in the realm of energy policy. I see five key areas as ripe for community intervention and structural change: (1) reforming the modern utility structure; (2) aggressive moves toward clean energy, including 100 percent clean energy policies; (3) net energy metering (rooftop solar) policy; (4) community energy policy; and (5) access to finance and alleviation of energy burden. These five policy areas are discussed in chapters 2 through 6, respectively.

We already have the tools to fight within our communities. We have been fighting for so long. Some of us have died, and others among us have averted death. We have marched for our civil rights, to be viewed as equal under the law. We have also marched with the insistence that our lives matter. The fight for energy justice is no less critical to the overall struggle for racial and social justice. Right now, we have the technology to lead to a fairer energy system, one in which the benefits and burdens are equitably shared. We also have the financing tools available to make the system more equitable, which is to say that we can ensure that those who have suffered the most within the current energy system will be at the front of the line to receive the benefits of the new system.

So, what are we waiting for? What holds us back from creating a new energy system? We need a revolution. The system of old shows signs of distress, but the only way to ensure its defeat is through a concentrated attack on the very policies that uphold it. The struggle to reshape this system must be fought not only on the streets, but in the interstices of policy. Poor people, Black people, Indigenous people, and those whose lives have been so profoundly shaped by the design of the current energy system must be the architects of the new system. The chapters that follow provide a field guide to advocates in the areas that are ripe for structural intervention.

CHAPTER 2

Utility Reform: The Linchpin to Transforming the Energy System

Before the conquest and unlawful annexation to the United States, before inequality plagued the state, and before the renewable energy transition, Hawai'i and its people had power.[1] Hawai'i's use of electricity predates the prevalent use of electricity in the United States. Hawaiian Electric Industries chronicles the advent of electricity on its company website, noting that King David Kalakaua's interest in electricity led to a meeting between the monarch and Thomas Edison in New York in 1881. Subsequently, on July 26, 1886, the king demonstrated "electric light" by illuminating his palace during the evening hours, to the thrill of onlookers and a gathering crowd. By 1890, three years before the US-led coup that led to the overthrow of the Hawaiian monarchy, almost eight hundred Honolulu residences had electricity.

Today, residents of the state pay the highest electricity rates in the United States. On Oahu, the most populous island and home to Honolulu, the state capitol, residents pay a little bit more than thirty-five cents per kilowatt-hour for their electricity. On the islands of Hawai'i and Maui, residents pay an average of around forty-three cents per kilowatt-hour. Compared with the US average of around twelve cents per kilowatt-hour, these rates seem erroneous. They are not.

The average Hawaiʻi household would pay more than $300 per month for electricity if its use were around the national average of 908 kilowatt-hours per month, but Hawaiʻi residents use much less energy than the average American.[2] When the impossibility of these electricity rates is placed within the broader economic context of the state, energy quickly becomes an economic issue.

According to the US Census Bureau, 9.5 of every 100 people in Hawaiʻi live in poverty.[3] When adjusted for the high cost of living in the state, the number jumps to around 13.7.[4] Practically speaking, that means that about one in seven residents in the state actually lives in poverty. Moreover, Hawaiʻi is the most expensive place in the United States in which to live. Improbably, the state is ahead of New York and California, states known for their high costs of living. Yet despite these disheartening numbers, the picture is not altogether bleak.

In April 2014, the Hawaiʻi Public Utilities Commission (PUC) dropped a bombshell. The PUC rejected the Integrated Resource Plan submitted by the Hawaiian Electric Companies (HECO, comprising Hawaiian Electric Company and its subsidiaries, Maui Electric, and Hawaii Electric Light), the state's 120-year-old utility.[5] The plan was HECO's attempt to provide a road map for the utility to meet the state's aggressive renewable portfolio standard, which, at the time, was among the highest in the United States at 40 percent renewable energy production by 2030. The PUC, the regulatory body responsible for regulating the state's utilities, issued its groundbreaking order just as the state was struggling to advance its clean energy goals. I arrived in Hawaiʻi two months after the April 2014 order, and its aims and articulated principles cast a long shadow over each aspect of the policies and debates that would come to define Hawaiʻi's clean energy transition: net energy metering, community-based renewable energy, the best business model for the state's investor-owned utilities (IOUs), and the shape of energy justice.

According to the PUC, the plan failed to grapple sufficiently with the rapidly changing landscape of renewable energy development in the state. As industry observers remarked, the HECO appeared unaware of the ground shifting beneath its feet; it assumed that, as a utility, it would be a part of any energy transition. The plan also failed to provide creative solutions to meet the state's energy needs or grapple with the utility's own mortality. When it rejected the plan, the PUC said that Hawai'i "has entered a new paradigm" where the "best path to lower electricity costs includes an aggressive pursuit of new clean energy sources."[6] The PUC called for greater creativity and invited the utility to devise another plan that would be more responsive to the dynamic nature of renewable energy production and delivery in the state.

For the energy policy wonks among us, the order represented nothing short of a call for a complete transformation of Hawai'i's utility, from one focused on profits to one focused on innovation in service of the people of Hawai'i. The order not only marked a turning point locally, but drew national attention due to its direct chastising of the utility for its self-serving efforts to slow-walk the state's renewable energy transition. The very last part of the order, Exhibit A: Commission's Inclinations on the Future of Hawaii's Electric Utilities, sent a chill through the utility industry nationwide and became the stuff of legend in the Hawai'i energy community. In the exhibit, the PUC made the unprecedented and unprompted move to challenge the fundamentals of the utility's business model, stating, essentially, that "we told you to make changes about a year ago, but you didn't, so we're about to call you out."[7] The PUC talked about the state's high electricity bills and burdens to consumers. The regulatory body articulated a vision for total transformation of Hawai'i's energy system through three key points:[8]

1. The utility needed to **create a twenty-first-century generation system**. Hawai'i is unique, but it has the opportunity to "leap ahead" of other states by "modernizing the electricity generation system to integrate clean energy resources that cost less" than fossil fuels. To do so, the utility would need to stop dragging its feet and "move with urgency to modernize the generation system on each island grid," stat.

2. The utility needed to **create modern transmission and distribution grids** that are capable of adding in more rooftop solar and other customer-sited energy resources onto the grid to "expand the array of energy options for customers to manage their energy usage[,]" including battery storage, demand response, and other ways customers can help to manage the overall electricity load.

3. Third, the PUC laid out a set of comprehensive **policy and regulatory reforms to achieve Hawai'i's energy future**, including fundamentally redefining the relationship between the utility and the customer.

At the time of the now infamous April 2014 "Order and Inclinations," the state was struggling mightily to integrate more renewables on the antiquated grid. The PUC believed that the utility was too wedded to the old, centralized energy model to create actual pathways for consumers to generate and store electricity. It explicitly asked the utility for a customer-centered business strategy and had serious concerns about "whether HECO Companies' increasing capital investments are strategic investments or simply a series of unrelated capital projects to expand utility rate base and increase profits appearing to provide little or limited long-term customer value."[9] Essentially, the PUC questioned whether the utility was simply out to save itself and pass on as many costs to customers as possible, rather than advancing the state's overall goals of a clean energy future. In regulatory parlance, these were fighting words, and the last state admitted to the country, a small archipelago in the middle of the Pacific Ocean, became ground zero for the national fight for the soul of the electricity system. The future of the utility business model was up for grabs, and the regulatory setting became the battle-ground for a transformation of the energy system as we knew it.

The Order and Inclinations was breathtaking in its scope and ambition. It read as a regulator's playbook for dreaming, visioning, and disrupting the status quo. It broke new ground and excited us all. We could see, in the PUC's words, a vision for a future Hawai'i energy system comprising customer-owned energy, battery-operated microgrids that could serve as mini power plants to the islands, and true freedom from the weight of the fossil fuel–based energy system that burdened everyone. And it wasn't just our future.

The question of utility reform and the regulatory secret sauce to achieve it now animates activist spaces that previously did not see the links between utility structure and social justice. In many ways, Hawai'i's PUC, with its groundbreaking Order and Inclinations, issued the opening shot. The PUC created a playbook for clean energy advocates and those who were simply sick and tired of the dominance and predation inherent in the investor-owned utility business model. For a number of reasons, the PUC's bombshell and ultimatum—"Utility, you must adapt to harness these renewable resources, or you will become obsolete"—resonated deeply with communities around the United States.

In many ways, Hawai'i was a microcosm of the issues imminently facing the rest of the United States. The battle between the utility and the PUC foreshadowed the battles that would begin to play out publicly in the wake of Hurricane Maria, which spiraled the already bankrupt Puerto Rico Electric Power Authority (PREPA) into even deeper chaos, and through the regulatory proceedings and the bankruptcy of Pacific Gas and Electric (PG&E), the largest investor-owned utility in the United States.

Many months before Hurricane Maria devastated Puerto Rico, PREPA, the territory's publicly owned utility, filed for bankruptcy protection. Hurricane Maria laid bare the territory's badly outdated and inefficient electricity infrastructure. The utility's financial woes made it difficult to develop a plan for restoration of power without also considering whether PREPA, as a going business concern, would be viable. As a result, in the months after Hurricane Maria, Governor Ricardo Rosselló put forward a plan to privatize the utility, essentially allocating parts of the utility's infrastructure to the highest bidder. In anticipation of receiving even less than the heavily discounted debt payments provided by the utility's bankruptcy plan, the utility's creditors balked at the governor's plan.[10] Local residents also voiced concerns about allowing the private takeover of what were essentially viewed as public goods. They feared that private entities would make access to clean, reliable energy nearly impossible for the territory's low-income residents.[11]

The California situation presents a more extreme case. Within the span of twenty years, PG&E twice filed for federal bankruptcy protection. The utility's first bankruptcy filing was the result of energy market manipulations by the fabled energy company Enron; the second, as discussed in chapter 1, was the result of losses caused by wildfires fueled by a changing climate and facilitated by the utility's failure to follow its own maintenance procedures.[12] PG&E's long record of bad behavior, particularly in relation to the wildfires that have plagued California, ultimately led to widespread calls for a public takeover of the utility, including by leaders in the cities of San Francisco and San Jose.

What lies at the heart of these debates surrounding utility ownership models is the understanding that the utility's business structure matters. Whether the entity is a publicly owned entity, like PREPA, a private, investor-owned business such as PG&E, or a collectively owned utility cooperative, structure matters. A publicly held entity may struggle financially, but ultimately remains accountable to the public it serves.

Investor-owned utilities are ultimately accountable to shareholders or, in the case of a utility in a bankruptcy proceeding, the utility's creditors. Cooperatives take the concept of public power literally. Electric coops are made up of members and managed by leaders voted into power by the members itself. In 2017, according to one estimate, investor-owned utilities provided electricity to 72 percent of the total utility customers in the United States, public power providers serve around 16 percent of utility customers, and cooperatives serve about 13 percent of utility customers (figure 2-1).[13] The question of whether we should migrate toward publicly or cooperatively owned power is a live one.

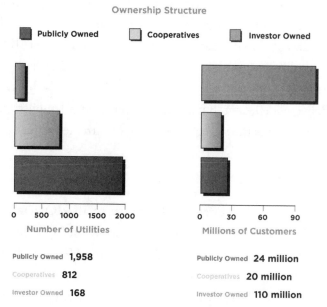

Figure 2-1. Breakdown of Utility Type by Number of Entities and Number of Customers Served

Source: Energy Information Administration, "Investor-Owned Utilities Served 72% of U.S. Electricity Customers in 2017," Today in Energy, August 15, 2019, https://www.eia.gov/today inenergy/detail.php?id=40913.

Investor-Owned Utilities

IOUs produce their own energy or purchase power through various power producers. Although they are only 5.7 percent of total electricity providers in the United States, they serve the majority of customers and make up more than half of overall electricity sales. Scholars and industry observers have identified a suite of problems commonly associated with IOUs during the energy transition.

As an initial matter, utilities are quasi-private entities incentivized to maximize investor returns. This built-in incentive structure can lead to high-risk, high-reward strategies for energy production. This structure may also encourage IOUs to externalize the costs associated with running power plants. Further, by virtue of their ownership structure and in the absence of proper regulatory incentives, IOUs are motivated by cheap capital, rather than altruistic goals such as mitigating or adapting to the impacts of climate change. Due to economies of scale, IOUs rely on centralized energy production centers that require electricity to travel great distances over aging transmission lines. Not only is this system of energy delivery inefficient, but as has been repeatedly demonstrated, this approach also leaves the system vulnerable to extreme weather events.

Public Power Providers

Public power providers offer an alternative to the IOU model, but their coverage is rather limited. Public power providers are government entities meant to serve the public. Despite being 66.6 percent of total electricity providers in the country, public power producers, such as municipalities, supply a relatively small overall percentage of total electricity customers.[14] The governance structure of public power providers offers some significant advantages in the renewable energy transition.

Public power can be less centralized, offering communities more direct access to energy decision makers and planning. The public ownership aspects of public power can lend itself to greater public accountability. The entity is "owned" by the public, much like a library or public school, so there is a greater incentive to engage in transitional energy projects or efficiency versus traditional energy projects or increasing energy sales. Further, a local board of local officials runs the utility, and its structure as a public entity lends itself to greater transparency.

According to the American Public Power Association (APPA), five tenets generally characterize public power providers: (1) public ownership—the utility is owned by and operated for the citizens its serves and is therefore accountable to them; (2) local control—a system of local governance and control over the utility's behavior, reflecting local values; (3) nonprofit operations—in contrast to IOUs, public power shareholders and utility customers are one in the same entity, which avoids the inherent conflict of interest that IOUs face with respect to excess revenues; (4) low-cost structure—access to lower cost tax-exempt financing; and (5) customer focused—sensitivity to needs of the local customer base, including the need for technological advancements and the mitigation of environmental concerns.[15] These common features offer opportunities for public power communities to shape their energy future in ways unavailable to those served by IOUs.

Regarding drawbacks, most public power providers are distribution-only power companies, which means that they must compete with larger utility companies for the electricity available within the broader energy market. This system places such providers in the same market with traditional energy producers, which means that public power providers could still operate to incentivize "cheaper" forms of energy production (for example, centralized, large-scale power facilities) as opposed to "cleaner" and more distributed forms of energy. In 2013, for example, public power providers generated electricity from a mix of sources: 17.3 percent hydropower, 7.6 percent nuclear, 39.5 percent natural gas, 5.4 percent oil, 28 percent coal, and only 2.2 percent of nonhydro renewables.[16] By contrast, the overall US power mix the same year consisted of 6.6 percent hydropower, 19.4 percent nuclear, 27.7 percent natural gas, 38.8 percent coal, and 6.2 percent nonhydro renewables.[17] Although this comparison puts public power providers behind the national average on nonhydro renewables, the transparent governance model holds promise, as a way to push public power providers more strongly in the direction of renewables. Despite the structural drawbacks that public power providers face in procuring energy, the cost of public power comes in slightly lower than either IOU or cooperative electricity.[18] As the APPA notes, public power utilities are able to offer lower electricity rates because their primary allegiance is with customers, rather than shareholders. They also face public scrutiny for expenditures, and rates are often set by public boards.[19] This scrutiny can lead to a reluctance to invest in clean energy or technology that may offer long-term benefits. Since state law exempts many public power providers from compliance with clean energy mandates, community members must stay active and elect managers who are willing to support public investments in local power.

Electric Cooperatives

In theory, electric cooperatives provide a panacea for energy justice advocates. Cooperatives are member-owned nonprofit entities that generally cover rural areas. Cooperatives themselves have existed for more than 150 years, primarily in the agricultural sector, and there are numerous rural electric cooperatives. Four features typically characterize electric cooperatives:

1. Democratic ownership and control by users
2. Limited returns on capital
3. Return of benefits or margins to users on the basis of use
4. Obligation that the organization be user-owner financed[20]

According to the National Rural Electric Cooperative Association (NRECA), electric cooperatives share the same set of core principles:

1. Open and voluntary membership
2. Democratic member control
3. Joint management of capital owned by the cooperative
4. Autonomy and independence
5. Commitment to education, training, and information
6. A commitment to cooperation among cooperatives
7. Concern for community[21]

As with public power providers, these core principles suggest that electric cooperatives are well positioned to foster an equity-centered transition to renewable energy.

As to their reach, electric cooperatives are only 27.6 percent of all energy providers and serve about 13 percent of electricity customers.[22] According to the National Rural Electricity Cooperative Association, the "905 U.S. rural electric cooperatives are independent, nonprofit electric utilities providing at-cost electricity to 42 million owner-members in 47 states."[23] In addition, "some cooperatives own generation. Others only deliver power from other coops, from independent power suppliers and/ or from electricity markets. They serve 12 percent of U.S. meters, own $140 million in transmission and generation assets, and deliver 11 percent of U.S. kilowatt-hours."[24] Property ownership is not a prerequisite to participation in the cooperative, and common benefits are spread over the group.

There is some evidence that cooperatives have met with success in advancing renewable energy goals and are more responsive to customer needs than IOUs. In Iowa, for example, Regi Goodale, director of regulatory affairs for the Iowa Association of Electric Cooperatives, said that Iowa's Farmers Electric Cooperative and Iowa Lakes Electric Cooperative "have figured out local solutions." Each cooperative, Goodale continued, "has a different approach to making renewable energy work for their organizations. And one-size-fits-all doesn't work."[25] In addition, a recent information guide distributed by NRECA states that, from 2010 to 2019, cooperatives increased their renewable energy capacity 151 percent.[26]

Regarding drawbacks, key concerns are governance, financing, and long-term commitments to fossil fuel generation. Given that members own cooperatives, governance is decentralized, which can lead to problems with ensuring that all voices in the collective are heard. Also, in parts of the United States where racial dynamics limit the political power and meaningful inclusion of people of color in decision-making, the cooperative might simply reflect the area's dynamics of White supremacy. The nonprofit status of cooperatives also limits the cooperative's ability to take advantage of federal income tax credits, putting such organizations at a disadvantage with respect to renewable energy development. Finally, many cooperatives have partnered to enter into long-term fossil fuel contracts, and getting out of such agreements would force the members of the cooperative to absorb the costs of contract cancellation.

The Problem with Investor-Owned Utilities

Let me be blunt. IOUs are deeply problematic. They threaten progress on both the clean energy and equity fronts. As discussed in chapter 5, the increase in locally managed and locally owned clean energy has pushed the modern IOU model to the brink. Utilities have struggled to keep up with the demand for customer-sited clean energy and have fought mightily to limit access to rooftop solar and community-based clean energy, disproportionately impacting the low- to moderate-income communities who need it most. The business model drives this injustice.

Utility investors expect the utility to maximize its profits by, more often than not, selling more electricity. The more customers who own and manage their own power, the less political and economic power remains for the utility, which threatens the IOU's existence. That is why utilities viewed the Hawai'i PUC's Order and Inclinations as such a threat. That is also why the order thrilled clean energy and public power advocates to no end.

Climate change and the extreme weather events it portends strain the IOU model. The IOU was designed to incentivize broad investment in the electricity grid. As discussed, the regulatory compact rewards utilities for investing in building more grid infrastructure by allowing utilities to pass along a reasonable return on infrastructure investments to utility shareholders. This incentive was critical to expanding access to electricity in the early twentieth century, but the model does not hold up under current conditions.

The IOU's built-in incentive to sell electricity as well as invest in grid infrastructure cuts against the imperative for customers to generate their own energy on rooftops and other community assets. It cuts against broad individual and community ownership of energy assets. The incentive model could also inhibit the ability of vulnerable communities to respond to climate change by prolonging reliance on vulnerable, centralized, electricity infrastructure.

The 168 IOUs in the United States serve an average of 654,000 customers each and provide electricity to the bulk of the country's electricity customers.[27] Despite their large national footprint and ubiquity, IOUs have also come to represent the face of the antiquated energy system. More than public power providers owned by government or community-owned and community-managed cooperatives, the IOU business structure cuts against the design of a clean energy future that empowers the most vulnerable. For decades, the business model has focused on keeping down utility costs and passing along as many permissible costs to utility customers as are allowed under the regulatory compact. Because they can access large amounts of funding to build energy projects, IOUs have doubled down on centralized, large-scale energy development that is inherently more vulnerable to climate change impacts. Further, their sheer control over electricity infrastructure and customers has made it difficult for advocates to access vital information to participate in regulatory proceedings on equal footing with utilities. Finally, the shareholder-driven business model of IOUs means that, more often than not, customers lose.

Concrete Strategies to Advance Equity and Justice in the Structure and Regulation of Utilities

We can view the concerns with IOUs in two ways. From one perspective, the concerns surrounding them reflect a structural issue that can only be resolved by a fundamental reshaping of the business entity itself. Proponents of this view argue for converting IOUs into public power providers, electricity cooperatives, or companies that focus solely on the delivery of electricity. The second perspective is that IOUs simply need to be regulated in a way that promotes the public interest. As law professor William Boyd suggests, the structure of the "public" utility has moved away from its initial form, which was primarily to serve the public.[28] Regulation could help shift the IOU back into the realm of the public service. Each perspective offers benefits and trade-offs.

Convert Investor-Owned Utilities to Public Power Entities

Advocates seeking a more justice-oriented utility structure frequently point to public power providers or cooperatives as viable alternatives to the IOU model. Since the early 2000s, several cities around the United States have explored the possibility of taking over IOUs to create locally controlled utilities more focused on deploying more clean energy. The municipalization process is complex and not without significant legal and technical costs, but in the long run it might provide much-needed local control over vitally important energy assets.

In 2010, the City of Boulder, Colorado, started on its path to local energy by declining to renew its twenty-year contract with electricity utility Xcel Energy. Xcel's resistance to increasing the amount of renewable energy on the city's grid had led to calls to turn the utility's assets over to the locality.[29] The nearly decade-long process for municipalization involved multiple steps, required stakeholder buy-in, and entailed considerable expense.

In 2011, voters agreed to fund a feasibility study to evaluate the requirements for locally owned clean energy utility. The city formed a transition plan in 2014, and opened a regulatory proceeding with the Colorado Public Utilities Commission (PUC) to facilitate the transition process. The utility resisted the city's efforts to municipalize and twice offered to settle with the city in connection with its plans. Three years later, the PUC issued a ruling requiring the parties (the city and Xcel) to reach agreement regarding certain issues in the proceeding. Subsequently, Boulder voters approved funding for the municipalization process, and the city council agreed to approve the legal process for the city to acquire the utility's assets. The city then moved for legal condemnation of the utility's assets.[30] Nearly ten years after its initial decision not to renew the utility's contract, the city had spent a total of $20.18 million on its municipalization project.[31]

Clearly, municipalization of an IOU is not for the faint of heart. For a number of reasons, Boulder seemed uniquely positioned to undertake the process. Its relatively small population and geographical footprint likely allowed the city to mobilize stakeholders for its efforts. Although the city encountered trouble in determining the scope of its bid for the utility's assets, the region's geography allowed Xcel's assets to be identified for condemnation from the broader electricity grid. Also, Boulder is known for both its affluence and its left-leaning politics, attributes that also probably contributed to the voter tolerance for such a time-consuming and financially risky move. For low-income communities and communities with less political capital, the municipalization process may seem a bit more daunting.

The APPA, the trade organization that provides resources in connection with public power, offers a resource guide for citizens seeking to municipalize their IOU. In the guide, APPA promotes public power as a pathway for local control of the energy system, to set local priorities concerning energy, and create a stronger local economy.[32] The organization notes that utilities often resist and "oppose the formation of new public power utilities because, for them, it means the loss of customers and profits."[33] Moreover, utilities see public power as a dangerous example of "what communities can do for themselves, and this may encourage other cities to form public power utilities."[34]

The APPA details steps toward locally owned and controlled power:

1. **Start with a leader**—A leader can be a group or individual who builds support for the effort within the broader community. The APPA notes that those "leading the public power initiative in your community should also be prepared to fight misinformation about public power: the incumbent utility may attack the concept of public ownership even before the city begins the feasibility study."

2. **Feasibility study**—The study should include an analysis of the economic feasibility of public power, including an analysis of the various power sources on which the utility might rely.

3. **Legal analysis**—The APPA states that legal analysis should include a review of local state law regarding the ability of a city to buy out an IOU's assets. Further, local law may provide an over-

view of the steps (condemnation of utility assets or a referendum vote, for example) to municipalize the utility. Legal experts should also examine the utility's contractual agreement with the public to determine whether it prohibits a public takeover of the utility.

4. **Valuation**—Proponents should also evaluate and estimate the cost of the entire electric distribution system. This valuation process will allow stakeholders to decide whether to purchase the IOU's assets or build from scratch, whichever is cheaper.

5. **Community education**—The APPA stresses the importance of keeping the public informed about the benefits of public power, especially given the likelihood that the incumbent utility will spread misinformation about the transition.

6. **Referendum**—A citizen vote may be required to authorize the creation of a public power entity. Where necessary, the referendum should include a question concerning governance.

7. **Price negotiation and condemnation**—The entity taking over the IOU should negotiate the purchase of the utility's relevant assets and should be mindful of the IOU's tendency to inflate the value of its assets.

8. **Public service commission proceedings**—Depending on the jurisdiction, the regulatory body may have the authority to determine whether the formation of the public power is in the public interest and the price that should be paid for the transition.

9. **Evaluation of financing alternatives**—Local authorities may issue debt or pursue other options for purchasing the necessary assets for the transition to public power.

10. **Prepare to begin operations**—The final steps of getting the public-power entity up and running include completing necessary contracts, setting up governance system, recruiting managers for the utility, and overall logistical planning.[35]

Promote Equity-Centered Performance-Based Regulation

When the possibility of converting an IOU to a public utility seems daunting, communities can instead advocate for performance-based regulation, or PBR, which financially rewards utilities for behavior deemed by regulators to be within the public interest. PBR connects to the idea that the issue with IOUs is not necessarily one relating to business structure, but a question of designing incentives to inspire the right type of behavior. Well-designed PBR can focus the utility's energy beyond selling energy and investing in unnecessary infrastructure toward activities more aligned with the public interest, but the process itself can be extraordinarily time consuming.

Community advocates should actively participate in regulatory proceedings involving PBR to ensure that the metrics used to evaluate the IOU's success incorporate the community's interests. The performance metrics should also be measurable and connected to the goals of the community. One metric might include ensuring that the utility decreases carbon and other harmful emissions within a certain, heavily impacted frontline community. Communities may push for increasing distributed energy access in low-income communities and communities of color. They might also advocate for greater access to community energy programs that result in actual wealth creation in their communities. The point is that communities must be a part of the conversation concerning PBR. The regulatory process should not be viewed as a forum to advance technical fixes, but one to incorporate interests articulated by the ratepayers whose interests the utility is meant to serve.

Although the PBR regulatory process may be daunting, it can provide a real opportunity for communities to nudge utility behavior in a more just direction. The end goal of PBR should be to align the utility as much as possible with the community's objectives of clean energy production and access to clean energy in the communities that need it most. The downside to PBR is that, at the end of the day, the IOU maintains its essential structure as a shareholder versus community-driven business entity with substantial control over all aspects of the energy system.

Convert Investor-Owned Utilities to Distributed System Operators and Energy Platform Providers (with a caveat)

The distributed system operator (DSO) and energy platform models offer additional possibilities for advocates seeking to transition the IOU away from its current role within the energy marketplace and more closely align its structure with the public interest. Under a DSO model, the utility can be rewarded for selecting not only the cheapest, but also the cleanest, energy available. DSOs can also be regulated to prioritize certain types of energy, such as community-generated energy, over other types. A distributed system platform provider, or DSP, is a close cousin to the DSO. As described by the New York Public Service Commission in its landmark 2015 order adopting a comprehensive approach to reform the state's utility sector, "the DSP is an intelligent platform that will provide safe, reliable and efficient electric services by integrating diverse [energy] resources to meet customers' and society's evolving needs."[36] Under the DSP model, the utility generally does not own generation assets but instead maximizes the value of distributed energy resources. As a utility executive explained, "The DSP is the air traffic controller of the grid," essentially moving different sources of distributed clean energy—like solar energy—where it is needed in the electricity grid.[37] A move toward these models wouldn't be too much of a leap.

Currently, some IOUs around the United States are what the industry refers to as vertically integrated utilities,[38] which means that they own electricity generation—typically centralized power plants located some distance from end users. They own transmission lines, the infrastructure needed to move high-voltage electricity across long distances. They also own the distribution system, the most visible part of the electricity system, in the power lines that attach directly to homes and businesses. The vertically integrated model can lead to perverse incentives for the utility, including squeezing out small-scale renewable energy generation from community energy projects. Moreover, this model has undergone significant changes, beginning in the late 1970s.

As discussed in chapter 4, Congress passed the Public Utility Regulatory Policies Act (PURPA) in 1978 in an attempt to deregulate the energy system and open up the three aspects of the electricity system for ownership by separate entities. Prior to PURPA, utilities had a virtual lock on all aspects of the energy system, but lawmakers designed the law to spark competition in the generation space and make more room for renewables generated by qualifying facilities.[39] As the Institute for Local Self-Reliance explains, PURPA "requires all utilities to buy power from qualifying small-scale clean energy producers when the price roughly matches what a utility pays to generate and deliver its own electricity, or what it would pay a third-party provider."[40] The 1990s saw a wave of "restructuring" of the utility market within most states. Restructuring allowed different entities to participate in generation, transmission, and distribution, which expanded the types of participants within the electricity system.

IOUs continue to sell the majority of electricity in the United States, but between 2005 and 2016, their overall sales dropped from 62 percent to 52 percent of the overall market.[41] New entrants in the electricity market—power marketers—have emerged to serve as an intermediary between the electricity generator and customers. Power marketers often offer lower prices for electricity than the IOU because their business model relies more on extracting a fee per transaction versus maintaining rates at a certain level to receive a regulated rate of return. In some states, like Massachusetts, Connecticut, Texas, and Pennsylvania, power marketers have accounted for more than half of overall electricity sales.[42]

These shifts in the energy marketplace raise questions regarding the ongoing vitality of IOUs and whether IOUs should shift their business model away from generation toward distribution. Some IOUs already serve primarily as distribution utilities, but advocates should push for the DSO model to increase opportunities for different types of electricity providers to participate in generation.

The caveat to this conversion is that although getting IOUs out of the generation game may offer more competition, it may be difficult, without regulatory intervention, for smaller generators to enter the electricity generation game. Even in the post-PURPA marketplace, corporate power providers with the ability to attract low-cost capital and sell electricity cheaply will win out over grassroots energy providers. In the long run, that could lead to more of the same: centralized large facilities owned by corporate behemoths, leaving smaller power producers behind. With this caveat in mind, moving to a DSO or DSP model could still help create pathways for more innovation around community-owned microgrids, community energy projects, and rooftop solar, quite simply because the investor-owned utility would no longer have a dog in the electricity generation fight.

Increase Opportunities for Community Choice Aggregation (again, with a caveat)

In the mid 2010s, community choice aggregation (CCA) emerged as an alternative to utility-owned power. CCA legislation varies by state, but generally allows communities to aggregate their buying power and bypass electricity generated by the IOU by procuring their own energy. CCAs typically are governmental entities or are run by third-party contractual arrangement. The local IOU maintains control over transmission and distribution, but the CCA procures energy directly from energy companies. This structure provides an opportunity for communities to negotiate directly with a power provider of their choice for their power.

Currently, nine states allow for the CCA model: California, Illinois, Massachusetts, New Hampshire, New Jersey, New York, Ohio, Rhode Island, and Virginia.[43]

This model appeals to communities seeking greater control over their electricity sources. As Al Weinrub details in his chapter on democratizing municipal-scale power in *Energy Democracy: Advancing Equity in Clean Energy Solutions*, CCA programs can offer a suite of benefits, including local control; investment in local, clean energy assets; environmental benefits; innovations around managing customer demand and energy efficiency; and lower energy prices.[44] To realize these benefits, Weinrub cautions against viewing CCA programs as simply a vehicle to purchase electricity. Instead, he argues for building a political "base centered in working-class communities, low-income communities, and communities of color."[45] He suggests that several principles can and should guide the creation of CCA programs: ensuring that local energy resources emphasize social justice and equity; enabling community ownership and control through energy democracy; creating clean energy jobs and family sustaining livelihoods; committing to workforce development and family sustaining jobs; promoting sustainability and the protection of the ecosystem as well as future generations; promoting healthy communities across a range of areas; including food access, transportation, and housing; advancing community resilience in the face of climate change; ensuring energy affordability and energy security; and acting with precaution in the face of social and environmental risks.[46] These goals and principles are what Weinrub refers to as "Community Choice Version 2.0," but the path to this more equity-centered approach to CCA contains some obstacles.

So far, affluent communities using the CCA model, such as the northern California community of Marin County, have opted for more clean energy than their local utility can provide, but that can sometimes come with added economic costs that are more easily absorbed by communities with more financial capacity.[47] Communities taking advantage of CCA legislation must also navigate a byzantine set of rules and guidelines and must have a fair amount of organization to even embark on creating a CCA entity. This complexity and the possibility of higher electricity prices can be barriers for less affluent, diffuse communities. They can mean that these communities miss out on opportunities to choose their source of power. Moreover, there is a risk that CCAs will leave the poorest communities to pay for the high cost of energy procurement by the incumbent utility, the same issue raised by utilities in the net energy metering context.[48] Still, the CCA model offers a glimpse of what might be possible with the appropriate legislative framework. More safeguards as well as equity-focused tinkering could make this model a powerful tool for communities wishing to avoid relying on incumbent IOUs for their electricity.

Pursue an All of the Above Strategy

The aspirational vision for Hawai'i's clean energy future landed in an exhibit to an order issued in a byzantine regulatory proceeding, but it created an opening to dream up a new energy system, unencumbered by the constraints of our current system. The Hawai'i PUC's vision—of a utility driven not so much by profit, but by the public interest and driving down the cost of electricity—along with its willingness to stake bold claim to the very possibility of a more nimble, just electricity system in Hawai'i, allowed me to imagine an energy system rooted in the principles of revolutionary power. We all have a stake in whether this energy future comes into being.

The strategies outlined are not mutually exclusive. Advocates can (and probably should) pursue an all-of-the-above strategy for utility reform given that the time lines vary from strategy to strategy. For example, regulatory proceedings and municipalization can take years and require substantial resources, whereas some reform approaches, like community choice aggregation, can be completed in a shorter time. The point is that the current utility model need not be viewed as a fixed part of the existing, unjust energy system. The structure of the modern utility system is up for grabs, and decisions around whether our power is provided by an investor-owned utility, a public power provider, an electric cooperative, or none of the above will significantly affect whether our transition away from fossil fuels centers justice. Utility reform provides an important starting point to achieve energy justice.

CHAPTER 3

Ending Climate Change Fundamentalism

To get to the small Hawaiian island of Moloka'i, you take a harrowing (in my opinion) twenty-five-minute flight from Honolulu, on the populous island of Oahu, to Ho'olehua, Moloka'i. On my first trip, I entered the tiny plane completely skeptical that the rather young-looking pilot had the ability to safely carry our freight of eight souls and untold bags and coolers filled with Costco goods, meat, and sundry items for daily life to the island. Although only thirty miles or so separate the island of Moloka'i from Oahu, the islands—and their respective cultures—exist in separate worlds.

Oahu serves as the state's economic engine and the gateway to the archipelago. The island's main attraction, Waikiki Beach, brings millions of visitors and billions of dollars to Hawai'i each year and dictates many of the political impulses emanating from the state's capitol in Honolulu. Although Oahu houses the majority of the state's economic wealth and political power, the island of Moloka'i, among the most economically distressed of the islands, is home to an unquantifiable amount of cultural wealth.

Many locals refer to Molokaʻi as "the most Hawaiian of the Hawaiian Islands." The full Hawaiian name for the island is Molokaʻi Aina Momona, which translates to "land of abundance." The 2010 US census put Molokaʻi's population at 7,345 people, with the majority of the people living on the island identifying as Native Hawaiian or Pacific Islander.[1] One community health organization serving the island estimates that 56 percent of Molokaʻi residents live below 200 percent of the federal poverty guidelines.[2] In 2019, that was around $60,000 per year for a family of four.[3] A 2000 study of food insecurity in the state indicates that 30.7 percent, nearly one in three, of the residents on the entire island of Molokaʻi live in a food insecure household.[4]

Basic items are hard to come by or are extraordinarily expensive. On those short flights to the island, visiting friends or relatives often bring groceries or other household goods to Molokaʻi residents. In terms of energy burden, in 2019 Molokaʻi residents paid an average of forty cents per kilowatt-hour of electricity, nearly 30 percent more than the thirty-one cents per kilowatt-hour paid by Oahu residents.[5] That puts the average Molokaʻi electric bill at around $162 a month, which reflects a usage rate of about 400 kilowatt-hours per month. Due to the island's exorbitant cost of energy, which is the highest in the United States,[6] Molokaʻi residents use around 20 percent less energy than the average Oahu household (who themselves use less electricity than the average American).[7] More than half—4.5 megawatts—of the island's 6-megawatt energy mix is supplied by diesel generators. The rest is supplied by rooftop solar.

Land on the 262-square-mile island is essentially divided among a handful of large landholders: Molokai Ranch, Department of Hawaiian Homelands, the State of Hawaiʻi, Puʻu O Hoku Ranch, and Kawela Plantation.[8] The history and cultural significance of two of these landholders—Molokai Ranch and Department of Hawaiian Homelands—warrant particular discussion. In 2017, the company that owns Molokai

Ranch listed the 55,000-acre property for sale for $260 million.[9] The proposed sale reopened the complex history of colonialism that seems more acute on Moloka'i than in other parts of the state. Up until 1897, Hawaiian royalty owned the ranch. The Cooke family then acquired the property and started a range of agricultural operations, including the American Sugar Company, beekeeping, and pineapple cultivation. The pineapple operations ended in the 1970s and 1980s, which also changed the economic landscape of the island.[10]

The lands managed by the Department of Hawaiian Homelands are a vestige of the unlawful conquest of the Hawaiian archipelago and the systematic dispossession of Native Hawaiians of their territory. In 1921, the US Congress enacted the Hawaiian Homes Commission Act, which established the Hawaiian Homelands Program. The program placed Native Hawaiians, who were "defined as 'any descendant of not less than one-half part of the blood of the races inhabiting the Hawaiian Islands previous to 1778,' on designated lands."[11] Essentially, the law created a pool of land to be held in trust for Native Hawaiians. The trust currently consists of more than 200,000 acres of land across the Hawaiian Islands, including the island of Moloka'i. Beneficiaries—Native Hawaiians with more than 50 percent "Hawaiian blood"—are eligible for ninety-nine-year homestead leases at $1 per year for residential, agricultural, or pastoral purposes.[12] According to a recent study, the demand for Hawaiian homestead leases "has consistently outstripped supply,"[13] and on the island of Moloka'i, the state is still working to develop the Hawaiian Homelands consistent with Native Hawaiian culture and values.[14] In addition, Native Hawaiians who are approved for the leases often face barriers to access the financing needed to actually build homes on the land.[15] Needless to say, the system is far from perfect.

I learned about Moloka'i from Malia Akutagawa, a colleague at the University of Hawai'i who serves on the board of a small nonprofit organization she cofounded, Sust'āinable Moloka'i. Akutagawa's family has lived on Molokaʻi for generations. She grew up free diving and spear-fishing into waters flanked by the island's impossibly high and sheer sea cliffs. She holds a deep familial and spiritual connection to the land on Molokaʻi, as well as a fierce commitment to the people of Molokaʻi who, on the whole, are poorer, browner, and more marginalized than people living in other parts of the state.

I landed on Molokaʻi in late May 2016, prepared to help host a community energy planning meeting organized by Sustʻainable Moloka'i and its then executive director, Emilia Noordhoek. We had invited community members and energy stakeholders from around the island to the meeting to share their perspectives on energy. We hoped to begin a dialogue about what community power might look like on Molokaʻi, the "abundant land," a place with the highest unemployment rates in the state and where nearly a third of the residents on the island's west side and one in five residents on the east side rely on food stamps.[16] Our meeting was also timed to coincide with conversations concerning a large-scale, privately owned solar project on Molokai Ranch. It also took place amid a resurrected discussion in Honolulu about constructing a transmission line to run the length of the ocean floor between Molokaʻi and Oahu to help quell Oahu's energy appetite.[17]

Noordhoek and I had invited community energy rock star Søren Hermansen, director of the Energy Academy on the island of Samsø in Denmark, to participate in the meeting. Hermansen is well known throughout the community energy world. In the early 2000s, he organized his small island of four thousand to become energy independent and actually supply its surplus energy to the mainland of Denmark. Through a series of clean energy developments on the island, including wind energy, Hermansen's tiny island has become an exemplar of the vast economic potential of community organized and owned energy.[18] Hermansen was keen to know more about Molokaʻi, and Noordhoek was keen to learn from him and his wife how they organized their island community for authentic community power. After our small group ate lunch in town, we headed to the quaint ranch house cum retreat center, Puʻu O Hoku Ranch, near the end of the road on the eastern edge of the island.

As we rode in a short caravan along the rugged Molokaʻi coast-line, I was anxious. My students would arrive later that evening, and I wasn't sure how our presentation, about Molokaʻi and its potential for community-owned energy, would land with our diverse group of con-vened stakeholders. The students had just spent the prior semester doing a deep dive into the Molokaʻi energy landscape, from its actual energy load and geography to its socioeconomics and politics. The students' work built on the excellent community energy assessment conducted by Sustʻainable Molokai in 2014,[19] so much of the audience would be familiar with the concepts presented.

At the back of my mind, though, I could hear the voices of so many people in government, industry, and even academia who had tried to dissuade me from mixing social justice concerns with the energy tran-sition. Their admonition was clear: energy is purely technical and has little to do with issues of justice or community engagement. In my core, I knew they were wrong, but after two years of hearing this message, the night before our big community energy planning meeting, I started to panic. What if I was wrong? What if the many deeply embedded socio-economic issues facing the residents of Molokaʻi had no nexus to the energy landscape? More distressingly, what if people didn't actually care about owning and controlling their own power? Indeed, what if energy and the complex regulatory system erected around it was too technical to merit interest from community members? I barely slept as these ques-tions rattled around my mind.

As with many important meetings in Hawaiʻi, before we began we asked for permission and a blessing from the ancestors to do our work together. Noordhoek had invited a well-regarded kahuna, or spiritual leader, to the meeting to offer a blessing. Our guests sat in folding chairs lined up around the perimeter of the room, some in rows, others against the wall. The kahuna entered the left side of the room, wearing very little, but somehow resplendent in his traditional Hawaiian attire. He was barefoot and held a staff. As he entered, the room fell silent. The curtains hung limply, and the air thickened. The man began to sing. He sang and chanted to the elements, calling them out by name, invoking their connection to his lineage. As he called on the wind, the very element that corporations and the state's investor-owned utility sought to commodify, the windows and side doors swung open. Nobody moved. He continued his rhythmic chant. We sat, mesmerized. He called on the rain, asking for blessings for the day. The sunny skies clouded over and the wind picked up, sending a misty rain through the windows and doors. The steady wind blew rain into the space, dampening the floor. He continued to chant. We sat. When he finished, every single hair on my body stood at attention. I caught the eye of one of my students, my face wet with tears. The sun reemerged.

We had permission to do our work.

Climate Change Fundamentalism and the Power Problem

What was clear to me in Hawai'i and has become increasingly clear to me in the years since is that energy issues weave into and connect with every aspect of daily life. We have an unavoidable and intimate connection to the energy system. Underlying social inequities magnify this connection. In a place like Moloka'i, where many of the residents already face food and housing insecurity issues, the high cost of energy dictates daily decisions concerning energy use and activities, such as keeping the lights on for homework, cooking a healthy meal on an electric stove, and using fans or air conditioners to provide relief from the summer heat. Moreover, the high cost forces a choice between paying for energy or paying for other items needed in daily life. These energy-related economic constraints plague many communities around the United States, but they seem downright paradoxical in a place with abundant natural resources.

The technospeak affiliated with most energy policy conversations surrounding the energy transition belie this intimate connection. More often than not, powerful stakeholders are more than content to maintain the false separation between the energy system and the social circumstances it creates because doing so avoids reckoning with the structural inequalities embedded within the system. In many ways, the existing system depends on structural inequalities, including extracting wealth from low-income communities and burdening them with the costs of the energy system.

The move toward 100 percent clean energy offers an unprecedented opportunity to redesign the energy system to mitigate the harms of the existing system. The transition also offers the chance for wealth creation in low-income communities and communities of color. The states seeking to make the most dramatic cuts in emissions and generate more of their electricity using renewable energy are best positioned to engage in this system redesign work and place equity and the economic empowerment of low-income communities at the center.

To make these changes, the laws and policies enacted to facilitate the energy transition must make explicit reference to issues of racial and economic justice. It requires that the most well resourced traditional environmental organizations—the so-called Big Greens—use their political and economic power to center marginalized communities, not only climate, in their law and policy advocacy work. It also requires that aggressive climate and energy laws pay more than lip service to equity concerns. Laws and policies must contain realistic time lines and mechanisms for effective implementation of equity frameworks. Finally, stakeholders implementing policy frameworks must dare to imagine a

range of possibilities for system design and grassroots economic participation in energy projects.

When I arrived in Hawai'i in 2014 on the heels of the Hawai'i Public
Utilities Commission Order and Inclinations, rooftop solar had reached
a tipping point. Nearly 17 percent of the state's utility customers had
solar panels, and the state's primary investor-owned utility, Hawaiian
Electric Company (HECO), had begun to sound alarms.[20] HECO
made two main arguments to try to slow down the rise of customer-
generated electricity. First, the utility argued that the electric grid had
only been designed to handle the distribution and outflow of electricity
and was simply ill-equipped to handle the large inflows of electricity
generated by rooftop solar panels. Second, HECO argued that solar
energy caused a "cost shift" away from affluent utility customers to those
without solar panels. The more nonpaying solar energy customers on
the grid, the utility argued, the fewer utility customers would remain
to pay the cost of maintaining the electric grid, a cost that the utility
had the legal right to recover from its customers. As discussed in greater
detail in chapter 4, these arguments came to be part of a playbook used
by electric utilities and promoted by conservative interests to put an end
to customer-owned solar, but at the time, they were quite new.

In my early conversations with Hawai'i community leaders concerning the state's energy ambitions and the growing conflict surrounding
rooftop solar, I was struck by a troubling disconnect between environmental advocates and social justice advocates. On the one hand, large,
well-funded environmental organizations seemed more frustrated by the
utility's attempts to stop the growth of the solar industry in the state than
by the actual need to address and resolve the underlying equity issues
raised by the utility. They were more concerned with climate change
than the social justice dimensions of climate change. Rather than see
the utility's arguments as an attempt to drive a wedge between low- to
moderate-income communities of color and clean energy progress and

try to address the real structural issues embedded in existing solar policy, environmental organizations only viewed the utility's efforts as an attempt to end rooftop solar. When I pressed some of these environmental advocates to think about ways to increase economic and racial inclusion in the solar transition, many people expressed the concern that equity was an untimely distraction, saying that a focus on equity issues at this early stage in the transition would unnecessarily take away from the state's promising efforts to increase clean energy production. In essence, they suggested, we should double down on rooftop solar as it's currently structured and worry about equity concerns later.

On the other hand, social justice advocates intimately understood the ways that the energy system impacted their communities. They also recognized the intense burdens associated with the cost of electricity, but they didn't see a clear path for participation in the energy transition taking place in the state. Issues like health care, education, and housing seemed to take priority over energy concerns, particularly because, from a policy standpoint, they seemed more accessible. Unfortunately, these issues are intimately connected to the energy system. A failure to deal with the costs and impacts of the energy system will only lead to more health care burdens, barriers to education, and housing insecurity. As I saw it, social justice advocates needed to be at the energy policy table or, at the very least, have their concerns addressed by those with seats at the table.

The unwillingness to include equity at the outset of policy discussions concerning greenhouse gas mitigation and aggressive clean energy programs perpetuates the wedge between environmental organizations and communities of color and all but guarantees that the concerns of marginalized communities will be left out of ambitious energy policies. In Hawai'i, I saw these dynamics play out on a microscale with net energy metering and the passage of the state's 100 percent clean energy law, but I imagined similar dynamics unfolding around the United

States as individual states made moves to adopt aggressive policies to reduce greenhouse gases and increase renewable energy generation.

What Is Climate Change Fundamentalism?

Gopal Dayaneni of the grassroots advocacy group Movement Generation calls the tendency to focus myopically on climate change mitigation at the expense of social justice concerns carbon fundamentalism. In a well-written piece published in 2009, Dayaneni argues that carbon fundamentalism is the "narrow focus on carbon reduction that only serves to exacerbate the root causes of inequity."[21] I have begun to refer to this narrow approach to climate change mitigation and renewable energy policies as climate change fundamentalism. No matter the lexicon, the sentiment is the same. If those best positioned and with the most resources to infuse equity into the debates on climate and energy fail to do so, inequality will be baked into the policies meant to transition our society away from fossil fuels. As Denise Fairchild and Al Weinrub write in their introduction to *Energy Democracy: Advancing Equity in Clean Energy Solutions,* "Simply decarbonizing the current economic system—hard as this might be—by transitioning to a nonfossil, renewable energy base does not challenge the fundamental logic or economic power relationships of this extractive global economy. It does not impact the growth imperative of the capitalist system nor stop Wall Street and the largest US corporations from extracting wealth from working people. It does not address income and wealth inequality. Decarbonizing this economic system extends its life."[22] And since the late 1990s, the tension between equity and environment has played out in important ways across the United States.

Implementation of California's AB 32: Climate Change Fundamentalism in Action

California's official greenhouse gas reduction efforts started in 2006 when the legislature adopted the landmark California Global Warming

Solutions Act of 2006, also known as Assembly Bill 32 (AB 32). This act sets aggressive goals and deadlines to reduce California's greenhouse gas emissions to 1990 levels by 2020. It requires a 30 percent reduction in greenhouse gas emissions from the then-projections of business as usual and gives broad authority to the California Air Resources Board (CARB) to implement the legislation through rulemaking. A cap-and-trade approach is at the heart of CARB's implementation of the legislation. Under this approach, emitters would be required to cap their emissions and purchase credits to reduce their existing emissions or, if their emissions fall short of the cap, sell their excess emission capacity.

Since 2006, CARB has presided over a multiyear stakeholder process to inform the rulemaking process and a scoping plan for implementation of the legislation. Pursuant to the law, CARB created an Environmental Justice Advisory Committee to advise on the process and ensure that the scoping plan included environmental justice concerns.[23] CARB approved the first scoping plan in 2008 and updated the plan in 2014 and 2017. From the beginning, the rulemaking process raised tension between the need to focus on the rapid reduction in greenhouse gas emissions and environmental justice.

Cap-and-trade policies allow polluters to decide whether to cap their own emissions or purchase allowances to pollute. Given the disproportionate number of dirty, fossil fuel–burning facilities in low-income communities and communities of color, environmental justice groups raised concerns that the cap-and-trade system might create or exacerbate "hot spots" in communities burdened by polluting facilities.[24] They worried that the older, less efficient facilities in their communities would find it far more cost effective to purchase rights to pollute than actually ratchet down their emissions, leaving their communities, once again, to bear the burdens of the energy system. They worried that the structure of the policy would leave their communities to shoulder the burdens of the energy transition, thereby replicating the inequality baked into the fossil fuel system. Unfortunately, studies released in 2016 bear out these fears and indicate that some environmental justice communities experienced increases in emissions after the adoption of the cap-and-trade policy.[25] Environmental justice leaders also expressed a deep desire to ensure that revenues from the cap-and-trade program be allocated to low-income communities, consistent with the law's requirements.[26]

Unlike most climate legislation, the California law actually makes specific reference to the environmental justice tensions at play in the move to reduce greenhouse gases. It includes a provision stating that the activities undertaken to comply with the implementation regulations "not disproportionately impact low-income communities."[27] In some ways, this language alone reflects a victory, but when it came time to implement the law through CARB's scoping process, advocates found themselves struggling to ensure that environmental justice remained an important consideration. Subsequent legislative action in California has attempted to address the environmental concerns raised throughout the CARB scoping process and the rollout of the cap-and-trade program, but an analysis of filings made throughout CARB's initial process reveals a missed opportunity for traditional environmental organizations to partner with frontline organizations at the outset.

A team of law students and I reviewed both the public-facing comments and scoping comments made between 2006 and 2017 by participants in connection with the AB 32 scoping plans. We cast a broad net and searched for any terms related to equity, environmental justice, and frontline communities. We also included conceptual terms that referenced overburdened communities, disproportionate impact, and broad justice-related terms, such as just transition. We were curious to understand whether the divide between large, traditional environmental organizations and environmental justice organizations was simply a matter of perception or if larger environmental organizations had engaged in climate change fundamentalism–oriented advocacy.

We focused on comments made by the Big Greens, a term coined to refer to the group of approximately ten national environmental organizations that dominate environmental advocacy.[28] Most of the Big Green organizations emerged in the 1970s in connection with rise of the environmental movement. They are well regarded, predominantly White organizations that routinely receive philanthropic gifts on the order of millions, as table 3-1 illustrates.

Table 3-1. The Big Greens

Organization	Total Revenue in Millions (2018)
The Nature Conservancy	$1,184.6
World Wildlife Fund	$256.8
Environmental Defense Fund	$210.6
Natural Resources Defense Council	$182.3
Sierra Club	$143.7
National Audubon Society	$133.5
National Wildlife Federation	$83.9
Greenpeace	$52.8*
The Wilderness Society	$42.8
Defenders of Wildlife	$39.1

* The sum of Greenpeace Inc. (a 501[c][4]) and Greenpeace Fund Inc. (a 501[c][3]) total revenues.

Other environmental, social justice, and environmental justice organizations also participated in the AB 32 scoping plan process. They include the local California chapter of 350.org; the California Environmental Justice Alliance (CEJA); the Center on Race, Poverty & the Environment (CPRE); Earth Justice; and Friends of the Earth U.S. Table 3-2 illustrates the stark difference in resources between the Big Greens and the other advocacy organizations.

We focused on the comments from both groups, the Big Greens and the other set of advocates representing a range of diverse interests.

Table 3-2. Resource Differences among Organizations

Organization	Total Revenue in Millions (2018)
Earth Justice	$80.0
350.org (national)	$19.2
Friends of the Earth	$10.1
Environmental Health Coalition (CEJA core member)	$4.2
Asian Pacific Environmental Network (CEJA core member)	$2.8
Center on Race, Poverty & the Environment (CEJA core member)	$1.8
Center for Community Action and Environmental Justice (CEJA core member)	$1.2 (2017)

Although it is an open secret that the Big Greens and frontline organizations frequently find themselves at odds in regulatory proceedings and legislative advocacy, what we found in our review shocked us. California has one of the most well organized and vibrant environmental justice advocacy networks in the United States, and yet, throughout the eleven-year process overseen by CARB, the climate fundamentalist–oriented comments of large, well-funded environmental organizations overshadowed the justice-centered comments made by smaller environmental justice and social justice organizations.

Between 2008 and 2017, in public comments related to AB 32 scoping plans, many of the Big Greens failed to mention equity, justice, and related concepts at all. The Wilderness Society, the Audubon Society, and Defenders of Wildlife fit into this camp. The remaining Big Greens either did not participate in the proceeding or mentioned the term fewer than ten times. This paucity of justice-oriented advocacy is only magnified by the statements made by other groups, such as Friends of the Earth and the Center on Race, Poverty & the Environment, which respectively made mention of justice and equity related terms and concepts seventy and ninety-four times. The California Environmental Justice Alliance's equity-based comments also totaled ninety-six.

The point of this simple counting exercise is clear. Well-resourced environmental organizations must not only step up their rhetoric concerning issues of justice and equity, but they've also got to put real resources behind the rhetoric. Doing that requires the Big Greens to advocate for equity-centered policy approaches in the proceedings that matter most. It means that they must develop a complex environmental analysis that takes into account the historic burdens that communities of color have faced. It also means that Big Greens should willingly be held accountable by the underresourced groups and communities who often lack a meaningful seat at the policy-making table. Finally, it means that the philanthropic organizations that generously fund the Big Greens should take notice: their grant recipients must embed equity in everything they do, particularly the advocacy activities that will change law and policy.

Bridging the gap between traditional environmental organizations and the environmental justice community is critical to ensuring that energy justice is a part of emerging laws and policies concerning clean energy and the transition away from fossil fuels. It is low-hanging fruit, given that the Big Greens and community-focused environmental justice organizations frequently find themselves in the same legislative and regulatory proceedings. Although some Big Greens have begun outwardly to shift their focus to incorporate equity concerns and principles, the hard numbers do not bear that out. An authentic alliance is needed now, as the new energy system takes shape through policy enactments around the United States.

In 2019, in recognition of the need for deeper alignment around racial and economic justice goals in pursuit of ambitious climate policy, a national coalition made up of frontline organizations and large environmental organizations developed a national platform to articulate "a vision for an equitable and just climate future."[29] The coalition's Equitable and Just National Climate Platform references the deep-seated and long-held tensions between traditional environmental organizations and frontline organizations. Its preamble states, "This platform lays out a bold national climate policy agenda that advances the goals of economic, racial, climate, and environmental justice."[30] Further, the platform "identifies areas where the undersigned environmental justice . . . and national groups are aligned on desired outcomes for the national climate policy agenda."[31] In a nod to the historical tension between the environmental justice organizations and national organizations, the preamble states that the platform "also lays the foundations for our organizations to vastly improve the ways we work together to advance ambitious and equitable national climate policies and to work through remaining differences."[32] Signatories include at least a few of the Big Green organizations whose goals have sometimes run counter to frontline groups, including the Natural Resources Defense Council and the Sierra Club.

Time will tell whether initiatives like the Equitable and Just National Climate Platform will actually advance equity-centered climate and energy law and policy, but an analysis of the early implementation of California's cap-and-trade law reveals a missed opportunity for such joint advocacy. The myriad debates on how best to implement rooftop solar reforms is another, as is community solar. In the absence of clear federal leadership on the issue of greenhouse gas emissions reductions and clean energy generation, more and more states will begin to adopt ambitious climate and energy plans. Big Greens must use their considerable economic and political power to ensure that this transition does not merely replicate the inequality of the fossil fuel system. If they are unwilling to do so, the family foundations that fund the Big Greens and their "equity" work must divert resources to those organizations that are actually willing to fight the energy justice fight. That is particularly true as Big Greens become more accustomed to using terms like *equity* in their public-facing materials to attract funders, but do very little to ensure that their advocacy centers the concerns of marginalized populations.

Hawai'i's Missed Opportunity to Center and Implement Equity Concerns

Hawai'i was the first state to adopt a 100 percent renewable portfolio standard. Act 97, adopted by the legislature and signed into law by the governor in 2015, requires that the state's utility procure 100 percent of its energy from renewable energy sources by 2045. From the outset, advocates questioned the meaning of 100 percent clean energy. Did it really mean 100 percent renewable energy? Did it allow for indeterminate definitions of "clean" that included things like trash incineration and natural gas burning, or was it truly focused on renewable energy like solar and wind? So far, trash burning counts as renewable energy in Hawai'i. Trash is considered biomass, but such facilities tend to be located in low-income communities of color.[33] Further, debates concerning how the energy would be calculated revealed that HECO's clean energy accounting system allows a power grid primarily powered by fossil fuels to achieve a renewable generation standard of 115 percent if customer-sited renewable energy, such as solar, is counted within renewable sales.[34] These details matter. They make the difference between whether a clean energy transition will truly benefit frontline communities or merely appease climate change advocates. Frontline communities and allies should force lawmakers to clarify these definitions during the legislative process.

Equity should also be a centerpiece of any legislative advocacy. Unlike California's greenhouse gas legislation, Hawai'i's law failed to make explicit mention of equity or social justice concerns. So, at best, advocates must now fight to ensure that issues of equity find their way into the clean energy programs and policies adopted to implement the state's 100 percent energy law. At worst, without a mandate, issues of equity might never be addressed at all. This dynamic played out in Hawai'i's complex community energy policy-making process (discussed in chapter 5) and is evident in the structure of the financing mechanisms the state has created to increase rooftop solar availability (discussed in chapter 6).

Without a clear equity lodestar embedded in the legislation for 100 percent clean energy, the state's most vulnerable populations will consistently lose. Low-income communities and communities of color will lose in terms of scale. Developers and utilities will favor large-scale energy projects that offer no opportunities for meaningful economic participation. Communities will also lose with respect to siting. Developers and utilities will continue to see vulnerable communities as sacrifice zones where large footprint renewable energy projects are located without the need to distribute economic benefits to the local community. Finally, communities will lose out on the tremendous opportunity to generate real wealth as a result of clean energy development.

A return to Moloka'i, the "abundant land," about two years after the community energy planning meeting we held illustrates these missed opportunities. In June 2018, the Hawai'i Public Utilities Commission approved a twenty-two-year agreement between Molokai New Energy Partners (an Illinois-based company) and the utility, Maui Electric Company (MECO), a subsidiary of HECO.[35] The agreement allows Molokai New Energy Partners to develop a 4.88-megawatt solar project coupled with a 3-megawatt battery storage system. MECO will pay the developer eighteen cents per kilowatt-hour for the energy it produces for Moloka'i's residents, and the company claims that Moloka'i residents can expect to save $60 per year on their electric bills.[36] The project consists of solar panels with a total capacity of 2.64 megawatts and fifteen batteries (with capacity of 3 megawatts) installed on vacant land owned by Molokai Ranch and leased to the developer.[37] According to the developer, the project is designed to store solar energy during the day and provide power from the battery system during the evening hours, when the island's customer-sited solar panels are not generating power.[38]

The project gets a lot of things right. The siting, or location, of the project is the result of years of consultation with local residents concerning clean energy. The project developer is an affiliate entity of Half Moon Ventures, a company that has long been interested in developing renewable energy on Moloka'i and has therefore worked hard to maintain relationships with community leaders on the island.[39] The project will, according to the developer, supply approximately 41 percent of the island's energy, which will go a long way to offset the existing diesel-generated electricity that MECO is working to phase out. The battery storage should also allow for vital backup power in the event of a weather-related event that knocks out power to the island.

The project also reflects some shortcomings. Although the backup power feature of the project adds a measure of resilience, the centralized design makes the project more vulnerable to power outages than a distributed generation design. Second, the project offers minimal economic benefits to local residents. The $60 a year projected economic benefits translates to around $5 month. For low-income Moloka'i residents living in one of the most expensive places in the world, this benefit will barely register against their $162 average monthly electricity bills. That leads to the final, fatal flaw, of the project: it offers no promise or opportunity for actual economic engagement or community ownership. Instead, in a place where the majority of residents are low income and Native Hawaiian or Pacific Islander, the state-of-the-art project merely offers a benefit of $5 a month. Sadly, on the island of Moloka'i, a resident might struggle to find a loaf of bread for that price. A focus on energy justice at the outset—by embedding it within the state's 100 percent renewable energy legislation—could have laid the foundation for a more equitable project.[40]

Ending Climate Change Fundamentalism: The New York Climate Leadership and Community Protection Act Example

The laws passed to require 100 percent or aggressive clean energy production within the next half century must be explicit in their recognition of issues of equity and justice. Since Hawaii's 2015 legislation, states and cities adopting similar legislation have moved in the direction of noting that energy and climate issues intersect with issues of equity. Significantly, New York's Act 8429, the New York State Climate Leadership and Community Protection Act (CLCPA), adopted in 2019, makes the aim of lowering New York's greenhouse gas emissions from human-caused sources by 100 percent from 1990 levels by 2050.

The ambitious law explicitly addresses issues of equity and justice and has faced scrutiny, praise, and critique. The law breaks new ground and reflects years of hard-fought advocacy led by New York Renews (NY Renews), "a coalition of over 180 environmental, justice, faith, labor, and community groups."[41] The "coalition seeks a sustainable future for the earth and all its people, recognizing that climate change represents a threat to all and especially to vulnerable people such as workers, people of color, seniors, youth, and the poor."[42] The group uses an intersectional lens to view the climate crisis and "believes that the climate crisis and the inequality crisis can be solved with the same set of policies, and that climate protection must serve as a means to challenge racial injustice and bring about greater economic equity."[43] The group's advocacy focused on reinvesting in "communities hit first and worst by economic inequality, climate change, and pollution" and made labor considerations a focal point of its work.[44]

Despite the many equity-centered provisions embedded in the

legislation, NY Renews considered the legislation only a partial victory and believed that the labor provisions concerning worker protections, job growth, and training got watered down in the final version of the act. Nonetheless, as the group's press release concerning the legislation states, "Legislators, executives, and government institutions must be pulled in the direction of justice by organized people, and that is what NY Renews has done."[45] Their advocacy efforts, which paired equity and environmental concerns, proved instrumental to the design of the law. It is too early to know whether New York's ambitious framework will yield substantial benefits for marginalized communities, but the legislation provides a strong starting point. The CLCPA can serve as an exemplar of tireless and strategic advocacy to ensure that climate legislation centers the concerns of marginalized communities. Advocates around the United States, particularly in states considering aggressive renewable energy goals, should make efforts to model their advocacy on the steps taken by advocates in New York.

Ensure that Policy Makers Recognize Equity as a Climate Concern

The legislation begins with the recognition that New York plays an outsized role in the national economy and, given the climate crisis, that the state has the goal "to reduce greenhouse gas emissions from all anthropogenic sources 100 percent over 1990 levels by the year 2050, with an incremental target of at least a 40 percent reduction in climate pollution by the year 2030, in line with" scientific projections regarding climate change.[46] The CLCPA also emphasizes the havoc that climate change wreaks in low-income communities historically burdened by the energy system; the legislation states that climate change "especially heightens the vulnerability of disadvantaged communities, which bear environmental and socioeconomic burdens as well as legacies of racial and ethnic discrimination."[47] The New York legislation charts a different path than Hawai'i's 100 percent legislation, explicitly noting that "actions undertaken by New York state to mitigate greenhouse gas emissions should *prioritize* the safety and health of disadvantaged communities, control potential regressive impacts of future climate change mitigation and adaptation policies in these communities, and prioritize the allocation of public investments in these areas" (italics added).[48]

Ensure that Legislation Includes Meaningful Pathways for Participation

The participatory elements of the CLCPA are extensive and detailed. The law outlines the establishment of a diverse state-agency-led council comprised of twenty-two members, including "the commissioners of transportation, health, economic development, agriculture and markets, housing and community renewal, environmental conservation, labor, the chairperson of the public service commission, the presidents of the New York State energy research and development authority; New York power authority; Long Island power authority; the secretary of state, or their designees."[49] The council also includes nonagency experts appointed by the governor, the assembly leader, and the state senate who must have expertise in climate change mitigation or adaptation, including environmental justice, labor, public health, and regulated industries. The council is required to convene a just transition working group to advise the council on labor-related issues, including workforce development, "with a specific focus on training and workforce opportunities for disadvantaged communities, and segments of the population that may be underrepresented in the clean energy workforce such as veterans, women and formerly incarcerated persons."[50]

The council's main objective is to create a final scoping plan through a robust, participatory process that incudes ample input from an environmental justice advisory group and the climate justice working group established through the legislation. The climate justice working group shall include "representatives from environmental justice communities, the department [of environmental conservation], the department of health, the New York state energy and research development authority, and the department of labor."[51] The legislation further provides that environmental justice community representatives shall be members of "communities of color, low-income communities, and communities bearing disproportionate pollution and climate change burdens, or shall be representatives of community-based organizations with experience and a history of advocacy on environmental justice issues, and shall include" representatives from New York City, urban communities outside of New York City, and rural communities.

Ensure that Legislation Includes the Distribution of Meaningful Economic Benefits to Marginalized Communities

Beyond the extraordinary participatory elements incorporated into the CLCPA, the law includes provisions for the distribution of resources. The legislation requires state authorities, "in consultation with the environmental justice working group and the climate action council,"

> to the extent practicable, invest or direct available and relevant programmatic resources in a manner designed to achieve a goal for disadvantaged communities to receive forty percent of overall benefits of spending on clean energy and energy efficiency programs, projects or investments in the areas of housing, workforce development, pollution reduction, low income energy assistance, energy, transportation and economic development, provided however, that disadvantaged communities shall receive no less than 35 percent of the overall benefits of spending on clean energy and efficiency programs, projects, or investments

and that the commitments outlined in the law do not impact investments already made in disadvantaged communities.

Advocates seeking to incorporate equity into ambitious climate and energy law and policy can use New York's example or refer to the excellent grassroots toolkit "Comprehensive Building Blocks for a Regenerative & Just 100% Policy."[52] The manual, available for free online, provides substantive recommendations on what 100 percent clean energy policy should include. The building blocks were created by a group of frontline advocates and people of color agitating for a just transition away from fossil fuels in various areas of the United States.[53] The authors ground their policy recommendations in "principles of justice, equity, and Just Transition." Their recommendations run the gamut and include a focus on prioritizing the needs of low-income communities of color, and ensuring that 100 percent legislation offers real health and social benefits for frontline communities, increases rural and Indigenous communities' access to renewables, and accelerates the distribution of economic opportunities in frontline communities.[54]

The move toward aggressive greenhouse gas mitigation through the establishment of ambitious renewable energy goals marks an important moment in the fight against climate change. The structure and design of these laws must reflect not only our highest ambitions, but also deep commitments to equity. Many of the other policies discussed in this book—rooftop solar, community energy, and access to financing—stem directly from the climate and energy legislation that sets a state's goals for the energy transition. When these energy transition laws do not center the concerns of burdened communities, advocates must fight the battle for energy justice on multiple fronts. Baking equity into sweeping climate and energy legislation up front will allow advocates to focus on the difficult work of design and implementation. The fight for revolutionary power begins at law-making and policy-making tables and will be more easily won when those best positioned to move the needle on justice issues embed a justice-centered energy and climate agenda into their advocacy strategy at the outset.

CHAPTER 4

The Fight for Local Power

"Water took like four months and electricity six. All that time. Six months is enough time for you to decide, 'I'm leaving here.' I mean, if it had been a month, you don't think so much about that decision. But so much time made a lot of people leave. And the more empty [it is], the worse it will be to organize ourselves to do big things because there won't be people to share the costs."[1]

This description of the nearly yearlong power outage across the archipelago of Puerto Rico paints a vivid picture of the ways the new climate reality intersects with access to energy issues and race. In September 2017, Hurricanes Maria and Irma descended upon Puerto Rico with a one-two punch. Up until that time, the islands of Puerto Rico formed part of a forgotten aspect of the United States' colonial past. They were US "territory" and long subject to various forms of exploitation, including widespread manufacturing for the pharmaceutical industry and bomb testing on the island of Vieques.[2] The islands are home to Brown and Black US citizens, but the residents of Puerto Rico lack the political power of those living in the states. Puerto Ricans have no congressional vote. The territory's poverty rates also place them among the most impoverished in the United States. The Jones Act requires that goods shipped between US ports be on ships built, owned, and operated by US citizens. This practice adds travel time and expense to goods arriving in both Puerto Rico and Hawai'i because, after docking in a port on the US continent, any island-bound cargo must be unloaded from foreign ships and reloaded onto a US-flagged vessel. As a result, Puerto Ricans pay the second highest rates in the United States for their fossil fuel–based electricity (after Hawai'i). Hurricanes Irma and Maria landed within this context.[3]

First, Hurricane Irma, a category 5 hurricane and the strongest storm ever recorded in the Atlantic Ocean, destabilized the archipelago's fragile energy system. Two weeks later, yet another category 5 hurricane, Hurricane Maria, made a direct hit. That storm cut a path of devastation that completely upended the energy electricity grid. The power outage highlighted the way that access to energy impacts nearly every facet of life. As one Maria survivor described these connections between energy and survival, "The people who live [in that community] are mostly older than forty, fifty, sixty years old. And sick people. Thank God [for] the owner of the business in the community, a lady in the community that had electricity early. . . . That business would buy ice and keep the medications, the insulins and everything, and all the sick people would put it in a Ziploc bag with their name, and she would keep them cold so the medications would not go bad."[4]

In the wake of the hurricane, individuals reliant on home medical devices scrambled to obtain generators to power life-saving devices.[5] Families lacked the ability to keep food and medicines cold. In the absence of widespread electricity to animate air conditioners and fans, the early autumn heat made life nearly unbearable for many and downright dangerous for the most vulnerable. For those in the dark for weeks and months on end, something as simple as streetlights compromised the sense of safety for communities and residents. Some communities found comfort and safety in their ability to come together. As one Puerto Rican resident recounted:

> We would put up lights on the street for when it goes out at night, at least for the first few hours . . . so kids could play and we could see them. We would come together in the street, play dominos. Sometimes we would cook together, just to make like everything was going great. So, let's say today two neighbors come and we did everything in our house, and another day they would invite us just so everyone could eat until we [could] find more food. We would help each other out, whatever a neighbor needed. We threw lines for electricity, just for the refrigerators, for the ones that didn't have generators. Mostly stuff like that, we came together as a community.[6]

But even with community solidarity, without electricity, schools and hospitals struggled to stay open, and many attributed the thousands of deaths resulting from Hurricane Maria to the lack of electricity *after* the storm itself.[7] A different type of energy system could have mitigated many of these harms.

As the world continues to warm and storms like Irma and Maria become more commonplace, the need for reliable, locally produced, and locally controlled energy has increased. Experts and advocates refer to this type of energy system as a decentralized (as opposed to centralized) energy system. Decentralization refers not only to the system of production and delivery, but also to the system of ownership and control. This type of energy system—a decentralized, distributed energy system—can be achieved in the form of rooftop solar energy systems or clusters of solar panels placed on critical infrastructure—such as hospitals and community centers—throughout a community.

For example, in Puerto Rico, the communities and homes with access to their own power sources recovered more quickly than those without. As frequently recounted in the media, Casa Pueblo, a community-based organization in Adjuntas, Puerto Rico, used its solar power in the wake of Maria to ensure that its most vulnerable residents had access to electricity for medicines and other medical needs.[8] The organization also served as a vital lifeline to residents needing to charge cell phones to reach loved ones around the island and elsewhere. In many cases, communities and individuals own the energy systems outright and are able to control distribution of the power to individual homes or areas needing electricity. In addition to control of the physical power system, in a decentralized system communities and individuals receive the economic benefits of self-generation of wind or solar energy. Rather than paying a large, investor-owned corporation to provide power, they own it themselves.

Although some might point to the vulnerability of Puerto Rico's electricity system as an anomaly, in reality the islands' system mirrors the predominant model of electricity delivery around the United States. In many ways, it actually serves as a microcosm of the design flaws embedded into the centralized grid design favored by the contiguous forty-eight states. The current, centralized system is designed around large-scale energy producing facilities that produce electricity in centralized energy facilities. These centralized facilities send electricity through high-voltage transmission lines to distribution lines that eventually power our homes. In many cases, despite the US government's attempt to create more competition within the utility sector in the 1970s, one company or a small number of companies in a particular geographical area still may control all the energy infrastructure, from the production to the transmission and distribution.[9] The climate future calls into question the viability of continuing this entire system, even in the wealthiest of states.

As discussed in chapter 1, for the past several years California, the world's fifth largest economy, has faced devastating wildfires that highlight the state's need to transition to a more nimble energy system. Three utility companies dominate the state's electricity sector: Southern California Edison, San Diego Gas & Electric, and Pacific Gas & Electric (PG&E). As in Puerto Rico, unprecedented, devastating weather events have compromised the state's energy system and exposed its inherent flaws, vulnerabilities, and inequities.

Just one year after Hurricane Maria struck, the Camp Fire, caused by faulty utility-owned equipment in California's sprawling electric grid, leveled the working-class Sierra foothills community of Paradise. The Camp Fire left many in the low- to moderate-income community without homes and, if their home was spared, power. The lack of electricity meant that even those *with* homes lacked the ability to power medical devices and cool food and medicines. For the most vulnerable, it meant leaving their homes in search of power.

The risks posed by utility-managed grid equipment are well known. Since the 1990s, sparks along the grid have set fire to overgrowth along PG&E's transmission lines. In 1996, PG&E was found negligent in maintenance of a faulty contact or loose wire, causing a fire that burned through 2,100 acres in Sonoma Valley and Napa County. In 1994, PG&E's failure to maintain vegetation in the area surrounding its electrical equipment led to a Nevada County fire, which burned through approximately 500 acres and took twelve homes and twenty-two structures.[10] Fire victims sued. PG&E was convicted of 739 counts of criminal negligence and fined $24 million. In 1999, PG&E failed to remove a rotten pine tree that fell on a power line, causing a fire that burned for eleven days and scorched 11,725 acres in the Tahoe and Plumas National Forests.[11] Multiple fires sparked in 2001 when heavy winds knocked over a pine tree that crashed into three PG&E backup power lines, leading to a settlement of $5.9 million between PG&E and 1,222 residents.[12] The 2015 Butte Fire was caused when a pine tree made contact with a PG&E overhead conductor. The fire burned through

70,868 acres, destroyed 921 structures, damaged forty-four structures, and resulted in two deaths and one injury.[13] Sadly, this is not an exhaustive list of the many fires caused by or related to PG&E's maintenance of—or failure to maintain—its grid infrastructure.[14]

In 2019, in the face of increased public pressure to manage the risks of wildfires, increased wildfire risk due to climate change, and mounting liabilities in connection with wildfires, California's largest investor-owned utilities enacted the euphemistically named "*public-safety* power shutoffs" (my emphasis).[15] The shutoffs mirrored the randomness and unpredictability of the wildfires and aimed to minimize exposure to fire risk by shutting power to certain high-risk areas of the grid. Rural and urban communities alike found themselves without electricity access and with very little notice to prepare for outages.[16] Some even referred to the shutoffs as a window into an apocalyptic future, noting that when the utility cut power to residential homes, it also cut power to the grocery stores and drugstores that provide vital lifelines to communities.[17]

The shutoffs affected hundreds of thousands of Californians. Once again, the vulnerability of the grid exposed underlying inequities. Californians already pay among the highest rates in the country for electricity, and there is some indication that the wildfire risk could increase this price.[18] In California's land of plenty, these economic burdens will land disproportionately on low- to moderate-income utility customers because it is they who typically pay the largest share of their income for electricity.[19] Just like Puerto Rico, the power shutoffs proved an annoyance to many, but life-threatening to those who relied on medical devices or could not afford to replace food purchased on a limited budget.[20] That these shutoffs occurred in the *absence* of actual wildfires only highlights the dystopian future that California, one of the wealthiest places in the world, now faces.

Unfortunately, the instability of climate change threatens most energy systems in the United States. Puerto Rico and California merely provide a sneak preview of our collective future. Their stories reveal that island communities, the poor, and communities of color will find themselves even more vulnerable as the climate crisis unfolds and that the design of the energy system is partly responsible for this vulnerability. The good news is that a design change can reduce vulnerability.

The current system is not accidental, so we can therefore *choose* to redesign it to align with the climate-related risks we now face, as well as principles of racial and economic justice. Net energy metering (NEM), along with community energy and more distributed forms of energy, provide viable alternatives to the centralized system. Solar power on rooftops could offer clean, reliable, and affordable backup power, as well as obviate the need for long-distance grid infrastructure that requires regular maintenance.[21] Solar power can also provide much-needed economic benefits to the communities and homes that need it most. Despite these clear solutions to the climate chaos we face, powerful interests have aligned to stem the growth of rooftop solar programs around the United States.

The Centralized Energy System: A Century-Old Design Past Its Prime

For the companies that participate in the centralized energy system, centralized power brings with it certain economic and technical advantages. For many years, local power companies have benefited from the utility compact introduced in chapter 1. As discussed, under the utility compact, companies are incentivized to invest in energy infrastructure and receive a "reasonable" return on their investments. From the early twentieth century until recently, this centralized system of energy production and ownership worked. Utilities felt confident investing in energy infrastructure with minimal economic risk. A centralized energy production system also made sense to companies seeking to maximize grid efficiencies. The technology of the twentieth century also made it logical to invest in large coal-fired power plants to maximize economies of scale.

Despite the mind-boggling complexity of creating a system of poles and wires to transport electricity, centralized energy production meant that energy delivery companies could concern themselves with fewer facilities, maximizing grid reliability and efficiency (despite some inevitable losses in energy potency along the way). The consolidation of physical infrastructure meant consolidation of economic power. The electrification process—dominated by a handful of large, regulated monopolies—therefore consolidated both economic and political power in the hands of a few companies with the technical expertise to manage the system. Decentralized energy production threatens this consolidation of power, and climate change destabilizes the guarantee of system reliability and the assumptions baked into the old electricity system.

Today, a centralized electricity system is actually more vulnerable than a decentralized system. When a major weather event occurs, the very interconnectivity of the electricity system means that vulnerabilities in one part of the system translate to vulnerabilities elsewhere. Moreover, a system of centralized power increases the likelihood that one problem can lead to a cascade of problems elsewhere in the system. Transmission lines can act as vulnerable nodes of power delivery; a problem with a transmission line may affect communities reliant on the system many miles away. A dramatic example is the Northeast blackout in the summer of 2003, when a tree brushing against a sagging transmission line in Ohio led to the loss of power for fifty million people across eight states in the United States and Ontario. The blackout—the largest in North American history—also led to at least eleven deaths and cost $6 billion.[22] Finally, the type of energy resources now more readily available due to technological advances—abundant wind and solar, for example—offer viable alternatives to centralized fossil fuel–based generation.

Decentralized Power: An Approach Designed for the Climate Crisis

The climate crisis illustrates the importance of a flexible and reliable electricity grid to the very vitality of marginalized communities. Access to distributed, local energy now forms a critical battlefront in the climate crisis, and it is playing out in one key policy area: net energy metering. NEM refers to the ability of a business owner or homeowner to receive credit on their electricity bill for generating electricity from (generally) solar panels mounted to the owner's rooftop. Federal law provides a pathway for states to provide net metering to customers through the Energy Policy Act of 2005, which directs each electric utility to "make available upon request net metering services to any electric consumer that the electric utility serves."[23]

For a number of reasons, utilities and those with ties to the oil and gas industry view NEM as a threat. In recent years, they have orchestrated a sophisticated and sustained attack against policies that offer NEM and NEM-like benefits. Frontline communities stand to gain the most from a cleaner, more distributed grid, but distributed energy cuts into utility and fossil fuel industry profits. The attacks on rooftop solar contribute to the deep inequality that these communities face when it comes to accessing clean, reliable energy. The attacks on NEM and distributed energy also threaten to increase the vulnerabilities that the most marginalized communities in this country face daily.

Access to solar panels, plus the ability to store solar power when the sun isn't shining, form vital components of a future where many more Maria-like storms exist. For those on the front lines of climate change— island nations, low-income communities, communities of color, and Indigenous communities—justice actually *requires* access to decentralized energy, as well as a mechanism, like batteries, to store it. As discussed in chapter 1, climate justice and energy justice advocates include this type of decentralized power under the umbrella of energy democracy. Energy democracy refers to the collective ownership, governance, and control of the electricity grid and grid assets, as well as the ability of individuals to have a say in the design of the system itself. Energy democracy holds promise as a possible framework for energy policies that help mitigate the vulnerabilities within the current, centralized power system. Despite the tremendous potential of and necessity for a decentralized energy system, utilities and conservative interests with deep commitments to the fossil fuel industry have made every effort to undermine local, decentralized power.

History of Net Energy Metering

In the late 1970s, states and the US government enacted a suite of policies to incentivize small-scale renewable energy.[24] In the 1970s and 1980s, global oil shocks spurred the federal move toward renewable energy. In 1978, Congress passed the Public Utility Regulatory Policies Act (PURPA) to, in part, increase competition and allow for alternative fuel service providers, "qualifying facilities" (QFs), to enter the electricity market.[25] The law defined QFs as small energy providers generating electricity from renewable resources, including biomass, waste, and geothermal sources, as well as energy facilities that produced electricity and thermal energy.[26] The law granted QFs a superpower: they could connect to the grid and receive compensation from the utility for the power provided. The law required that the utility pay a QF for both the energy produced and the QF's "capacity," or potential output, at the utility's "avoided cost." The avoided cost "is what it would have cost the utility to generate or contract for the energy and capacity in the absence of the QF."[27] In many ways, PURPA blew the electric industry apart. The law provided valuable incentives for more diverse players to enter the market and do so with clean energy generation. PURPA also paved the way for rooftop solar.

In the late 1990s, states began to adopt increasingly aggressive renewable energy goals, called renewable portfolio standards. To incentivize renewable energy production and diversify energy sources, certain states passed laws to facilitate NEM.[28] Under a traditional NEM program, for every kilowatt-hour produced on a participant's rooftop, the participant receives a one-for-one credit against the participant's electricity bill. Rather than compensating the rooftop solar customer for the rate the utility pays for producing or acquiring the kilowatt-hour (the avoided cost), traditional rooftop solar programs compensate customers at the "retail rate" for electricity, which is the same price that the utility sells the electricity to the customer. This critical pricing mechanism made rooftop solar economically feasible for early adopters. In addition to "turning electricity meters back to zero," some state NEM programs allow participants to sell any excess energy back into the grid, providing yet a further economic incentive for solar adoption.

Solar Financing and Distribution of Economic Benefits

Panels purchased in the early days of NEM were expensive, and early adopters tended to be affluent homeowners or business owners.[29] Gradually, in addition to providing panels to customers who could purchase them outright, solar companies began to offer lease options to minimize panel costs for those interested in generating solar energy from their rooftops, but who could not pay the upfront costs; banks also began to offer financing options for those who wanted to purchase solar panels and pay down the cost over time. States and cities also offered their own range of incentives to increase rooftop solar penetration.[30] The federal government also created a financial incentive to homeowners and solar companies through investment tax credits, or ITCs, which payed a percentage—typically 30 percent—of the cost of the overall solar panel investment back to an investor in the form of a credit against the investor's tax bill. When the homeowner owns the panels, the homeowner receives the ITC; if the solar company owns the system, the company receives the credit. By virtue of its structure, the ITC helped generate additional wealth for those with means.

In terms of actual bill benefits, when a solar customer finances the panels through her bank, the customer pays down the cost of the panels through a loan. She receives the retail rate of exchange for the energy she produces, ultimately reducing her electricity bill to zero (or "turning back the meter"). Under the bank-financed option, the customer is also eligible for the ITC.

With the solar leasing model, the solar company receives the bulk of the economic benefits, including the full retail rate of exchange for electricity it produces, and any tax or other incentives (such as marketable renewable energy credits) offered by state and federal governments. Solar customers leasing panels from solar companies receive less than the one-for-one retail rate of exchange offered by most NEM programs, but solar companies typically offer customers a better deal on their electricity than the utility. In exchange for financing the panels through the company, the company passes on energy bill savings to the solar customer at a fixed rate. Rather than paying the full retail price for electricity, the customer might receive a slight discount on their bill. All that is done pursuant to a "power purchase agreement" entered into between the solar company and the solar customer for power over a fixed amount of time and an interconnection agreement between the solar company and the utility. Eventually, at the termination of the power purchase agreement, the rooftop solar customer may decide to purchase the panels outright, which gives the customer (rather than the solar company) the right to receive a one-for-one credit on her electricity bill.

In the 2010s, the cost of solar panels dropped so much that those who initially saw solar as out of reach began to contemplate either purchasing solar panels outright or participating in a solar company financing program.[31] Middle-class families—and those with moderate incomes—saw solar not only as something to help reduce global greenhouse gas emissions, but also as a way to cut down on electricity bills with only a modest investment. With lower barriers to entry, solar became a good deal. States like Hawai'i and Nevada saw such high solar adoption rates that utilities, and stakeholders deeply embedded within the fossil fuel industry, took notice. This success led to the systematic dismantling of rooftop solar programs around the United States—starting in the sunny states of Hawai'i, Nevada, and Arizona—led by powerful interests who stood to lose the most within a system of decentralized power.

Solar and Race

Before getting into the playbook designed by utility companies and powerful corporate interests to dismantle distributed energy around the United States, we have to talk about race. As mentioned, early rooftop solar programs were only accessible to the wealthy. Because class divisions frequently line up with racial inequities, one might stereotype these early solar adopters as ardent White environmentalists determined to use their resources to curb the threat of global warming. And, given that early environmentalists were frequently critiqued by frontline communities for caring more about saving the whales than their fellow humans breathing in the toxic fumes of a power plant, it is not a stretch to stereotype solar adopters as caring little about equity concerns. Conservative interest groups play on and exploit these long-standing dynamics and stereotypes, which themselves are deeply rooted in the historical tensions between racial minorities and the environmental movement.

Stereotypes notwithstanding, the truth is that solar *has* been adopted along racial lines. Recent studies show that, even as the price of solar has dropped, a racial disparity persists.[32] A 2019 study of rooftop solar penetration around the United States showed that, even when controlling for home ownership and income, Black and Brown communities have fewer rooftop solar panels than White communities.[33] The study's authors attribute this finding to a number of possibilities, such as "seeding," which occurs when one neighbor gets solar panels and others in the neighborhood, seeing solar as an option, look into putting panels on their rooftops.

Some might also attribute the disparity in solar adoption to good old-fashioned racism. The solar industry is itself a fairly White industry, and White solar customers may be seen as low-hanging fruit. Cultural stereotypes concerning traditional environmentalism, as well as racist notions of who pays bills on time, could very well contribute to the lower adoption rates in communities of color. No matter the reason for low adoption rates in communities of color, utilities and fossil fuel interests have exploited the racial wedge.

The Playbook to Slow Solar Adoption

The utility industry and those with deep roots in the fossil fuel business are using NEM as a racially divisive tool to divide White communities and communities of color. Now that rooftop solar is on the rise and becoming more accessible to low- to moderate-income ratepayers in marginalized communities, utilities and the conservative think tank financed by doyens of the fossil fuel industry, the American Legislative Exchange Council (ALEC), are doing everything they can to limit wider adoption.[34] They have deployed what I call the playbook to systematically dismantle existing rooftop solar programs in sunny states, as well as prevent the growth of rooftop solar in some of the poorest states, where utility customers could benefit the most.

The playbook involves the core arguments provided in a 2013 filing before the Arizona Corporation Commission by Arizona's investor-owned utility, Arizona Public Service (APS), seeking to restructure the state's NEM program. As stated in APS's application to the state, "The incentive embedded in Net Metering . . . does not reflect the value that solar generation provides to the electric system. . . . Net Metering allows customers installing rooftop solar to avoid paying for infrastructure they rely on and services they use, [and] these installations come at a cost to APS's remaining non-solar customers."[35]

In an ingenious move, the playbook's authors exploit the racial history of the United States, arguing that "those (White)" people are benefiting from a system that leaves "you (Black and Brown people)" out. In essence, the playbook suggests that solar adopters are getting away with something at the expense of those without solar. They are getting more than they deserve, and this, the playbook suggests, is patently unfair. The system is unfair; it was unfair from the beginning; and if we don't act now, it will forever be unfair. Therefore, the playbook states, let's dismantle rooftop solar and make sure that no one is unfairly burdened by the energy system because, the subtext goes, "We (the utility) have always cared about the most vulnerable in the system." Playbook proponents not only say all the foregoing with a straight face, but they also make these arguments in documents filed publicly with regulators all over the United States.

In addition to the "fairness" and "equity" concepts that lurk throughout the playbook, it also frequently mentions the undue strain that rooftop solar causes on the electricity grid. Because the grid was designed to be a one-way system that delivers electricity *to* homes, rather than receives electricity *from* homes, intermittent rooftop solar power will essentially break the grid.

In a smattering of regulatory proceedings designed to remedy the overall "unfairness" of current NEM programs and avoid grid collapse, users of the playbook have taken three related tacks. First, playbook users (typically utilities and utility supporters) urge regulators to simply decrease the exchange rate offered to rooftop solar customers to align it with the "wholesale" or "avoided cost" of energy. In some states, this reduction might be a nearly two-thirds reduction in the exchange rate;

for example, the rate given to solar customers for their electricity might go from fifteen cents per kilowatt-hour to six cents per kilowatt-hour. This treats solar customers like utilities rather than prosumers providing added benefits to the grid.[36]

Second, playbook proponents argue for an increase in the amount of fixed charges that can be passed on to utility customers. This increase, they argue, would be done to offset the unfair "cost shifts" to nonparticipating utility customers and ensure that solar customers are paying their fair share for their use of the grid. This additional fee can also help utilities accommodate and prepare for the potential grid collapse danger posed by intermittent rooftop solar energy. Unfortunately, this fixed fee would be regressive and place disproportionate economic burdens on low-income ratepayers.

A final, third tactic deployed by proponents of the playbook is to upend the entire system of reimbursing solar customers for the electricity they produce. In this tactic, playbook users argue that the real "value of solar" is significantly less than the exchange rate rooftop solar customers have historically received, and so the overall compensation rate offered to rooftop solar customers (the retail rate) should ultimately be reduced to the utility's avoided cost associated with deploying a customer's rooftop energy. This third tactic has led at least twenty-eight jurisdictions around the United States to initiate complex "value of solar" proceedings to determine the precise value of solar energy to the electricity grid and whether the compensation rate should be reduced.[37]

Despite the premise that rooftop solar harms low-income people of color, all three tactics—reducing the exchange rate for solar energy, increasing fixed costs on energy bills, and initiating value of solar proceedings—actually harm marginalized communities. First, reducing the exchange rate makes solar less attractive to those who, due to the drop in the price of solar panels, can now afford it. In the past, the cost of solar panels eventually paid for itself. Why should those with fewer economic resources pay a premium for solar energy now? Second, increasing fixed costs on utility bills harms those on low and fixed incomes. Given the significant energy burdens that low- to moderate-income utility customers already face, adding fees to their electricity bills poses a significant hardship.

Finally, value of solar proceedings reflect an attempt to scale back the compensation rate provided to rooftop solar adopters to align with the avoided cost rate, which will—as with the first tactic—lead to lower solar adoption rates in marginalized communities. In value of solar proceedings, the playbook disaggregates the cost of fuel service into quantifiable layers that are "stacked" into a value that adds up to the amount customers pay for electricity. The stack is meant to visually reflect the costs that the utility will avoid by deploying rooftop solar energy and tally up to the "fair" solar exchange rate. The playbook suggests that solar customers should only receive compensation for defraying the utility's generation costs, not the other fixed costs of maintaining the electricity system.

The "value stack" analysis includes things like fuel costs and transmission costs, but rooftop solar provides intangible benefits that do not neatly fit into the stack. The value stack promoted in the playbook leaves out the incredible social and environmental costs that are avoided by using solar energy. Although some regulators and states have started to include the "social value of solar" in proceedings connected to the value of solar, the playbook is typically the starting place. Without careful vigilance and advocacy to expand the values included in the stack, value of solar proceedings can unfairly obscure the less tangible benefits of solar.

The "value stacking" approach is now the dominant approach taken by regulators examining the value of solar, and it unfairly limits the scope of the debate at the outset. The focus on what "value" the solar energy adds to the grid also puts the burden on solar advocates, as well as low- to moderate-income customers, to argue that things like social and environmental benefits should add to the overall value of rooftop solar. Beyond the health and environmental benefits of clean distributed energy, regulators should also look to grid resilience—the ability of the grid to withstand climate shocks—which is so very critical in the climate era. This, too, should boost the value designated for solar.

As a lawyer, I am all too familiar with the idea that the framer of the debate itself has the power to dictate the terms of the debate (any transactional lawyer will always want to be the first drafter; if you have a choice, don't let them). What ALEC and the utility industry have seized on is a debate frame, thinly veiled by references to "equity" and "fairness," that actually fails to deal with the many, many unquantified costs and burdens that low-income communities and communities of color have weathered so as to keep on their neighbors' lights in the fossil fuel era. None of the utility or industry filings that I have reviewed indicates a desire to remedy *that* harm. That is what is at stake in this fight.

Despite its widespread adoption in rooftop solar and related "value of solar" proceedings around the United States, the playbook misses the mark. Upon examination, the playbook is merely a racial dog whistle to communities who have long distrusted the energy system due to its disproportionate harmful impacts. Moreover, the playbook is myopic. Any party concerned with burdens should start with the energy system costs historically borne by low-income communities and communities of color and then look at future costs to generations that will be impacted by climate change. The communities who will suffer the most from climate change are those who stand to gain the most from broadening access to rooftop solar in their communities today. The playbook's pandering to equity is downright disingenuous. The three primary tactics that define the playbook will hurt the very people that playbook users claim to care about—low- to moderate-income ratepayers—the most.

Conservative Advocacy to Dismantle Rooftop Solar Programs

It does not help that the utility industry has its own conservative legislative advocacy organization, in the form of ALEC, to parrot its demands. ALEC is a well-financed and well-resourced legislative think tank that advances conservative causes. The group has long been associated with the fossil fuel industry and the corporations that rain pollution down on low-income communities and communities of color.

The intimate connections between ALEC and the utility industry are clear. For example, while researching material for this book, my research team and I uncovered identical charts used by both the utility industry and ALEC to advocate for the curtailment of NEM. In the July 12, 2013, filing by APS referenced earlier, APS used two key figures to argue that solar customers do not pay their fair share for grid maintenance. The first figure, "Typical Grid Interaction for Rooftop Solar," illustrates the typical electricity generation curve for a solar customer. See figure 4-1. The image is meant to reflect the solar customer's heavy reliance on the grid and to support the argument that solar customers should receive less compensation for the solar energy they produce.

In the middle of the day, between 12 p.m. and 4 p.m., the figure indicates, the customer's electricity generation covers the customer's electricity use, and the customer is able to export excess generation the customer produces to other utility customers. Under the customer's generation curve is a note, "Customer generation, grid support needed." In the portion of the curve showing the customer exporting extra energy to the grid, the chart notes, "Customer uses grid to export excess power."[38] On either side of the customer generation curve are the remaining hours of the day when, in the utility's filing, "APS provides power."[39] The chart comes straight out of the playbook.

ALEC uses the exact chart in its report "Reforming Net Metering:

Providing a Bright and Equitable Future," published in March 2014 and written by Tom Tanton. In ALEC's report, the solar customer chart used by APS appears under a new title, "Typical Energy Production and Consumption for a Small Customer with Solar PV," but the details and images are identical. The bottom line is that solar customers who receive a one-for-one retail rate exchange for the energy they produce are unfairly burdening the rest of the utility's customers and relying on grid services without paying for them. The use of identical charts in ALEC's report and the utility's regulatory proceeding reveals a cozy relationship between the fossil fuel interests and the utility sector. It should also raise red flags concerning the authenticity of a utility's race-based

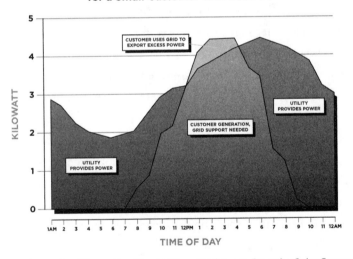

Figure 4-1. Example of Figure Used by ALEC and Utilities to Describe Solar Customer's Use of the Electric Grid

Sources: "Application of the Arizona Public Service Company before the Arizona Corporation Commission in Docket E-01345A-13-0248," July 12, 2013; Tom Tanton, "Reforming Net Metering: Providing a Bright and Equitable Future," American Legislative Exchange Council, March 2014, https://www.alec.org/app/uploads/2015/12/2014-Net-Metering-reform-web.pdf, 17.

advocacy against NEM. Figure 4-1 reproduces the image used across ALEC's and APS's materials.

The second figure that appears in both reports relates to the value-based arguments raised in regulatory proceedings. The image lends support to the argument that solar unfairly extracts more from the grid than it gives. See figure 4-2.

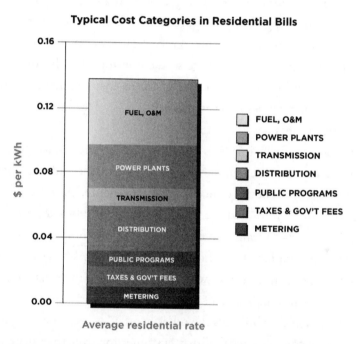

Figure 4-2. Example of Figure Used by ALEC and Utilities to Reflect Value Stack

Sources: "Application of the Arizona Public Service Company before the Arizona Corporation Commission in Docket E-01345A-13-0248," July 12, 2013; Tom Tanton, "Reforming Net Metering: Providing a Bright and Equitable Future," American Legislative Exchange Council, March 2014, https://www.alec.org/app/uploads/2015/12/2014-Net-Metering-reform-web.pdf, 17.

In APS's filing, the utility names the figure "Typical Cost Categories in Residential Bill," which is similar to ALEC's figure, "California Rate Components." Both charts show what goes into a typical customer's electricity bill through a series of layers. In ALEC's example, the rate ultimately paid by customers includes generation, distribution, the cost of transmission, the cost of public purpose programs (serving low-income customers), the cost of nuclear decommissioning, payback for energy recovery bonds sold by California utility during the state's energy crisis, and payback to the state's Department of Water Resources for bonds issued during the state's 2001 energy crisis. Arizona's example includes the cost of metering, taxes and government fees, public programs, cost of distribution, cost of transmission, cost of power plants, and cost of fuel. In both charts, the costs are stacked on top of each other to add up to the overall retail rate. In the California example, the retail rate is around fifteen cents per kilowatt-hour; in Arizona, the rate is around the same, fifteen cents per kilowatt-hour.

The point of the image is to suggest that when solar customers receive at or near full retail credit—fifteen cents per kilowatt-hour—for the electricity they produce from their rooftop, they receive more than what they are providing: fuel. The utility would like to take one slice of the stack—ideally generation—and solely compensate the solar customer for helping the utility to avoid that cost. Under the utility's approach, the solar customer would receive far less in exchange for the electricity she produces and essentially pay for the other things typically included in a utility bill. On the other hand, playbook users argue that if the utility compensates the solar customer for *more* than generation, the overcompensation operates as a "cost shift" to customers who are, according to the argument, effectively subsidizing the solar customer by absorbing the costs the rooftop solar customer is not paying. In effect, under this arrangement "other power customers are subsidizing the higher payments that utilities make for power purchases. . . . "[40] This is the essence of the "cost-shift" argument. For example, in its regulatory filing, APS argues that, on average, the "cost shift each year is approximately $1,000 per rooftop solar system. That means higher electricity rates for customers without solar. This cost shift is unfair." The utility goes on, noting "and as more customers install solar, the cost shift will continue to grow."

All this unfairness ultimately leads to one conclusion, according to the playbook. The imbalance in the exchange rate will ultimately create a shortfall in the utility's balance sheet, forcing the utility to raise rates on other, nonsolar customers so as to cover the "fixed costs" of maintaining the grid.[41] This is the so-called utility death spiral. The theory provides that the more solar customers there are, the more expensive electricity will be for those without solar, which will lead more and more customers to see solar as an economically viable choice and leave the grid, which will lead to more expensive electricity for those who remain grid tied, and so on. The underlying fear, articulated well in a 2013 utility industry paper, "Disruptive Challenges: Financial Implications and Strategic Responses to a Changing Retail Electric Business," is that the utility will eventually lose a base sufficient to support its operations[42] (and, of course, be unable to provide shareholders with the return on their investment they've come to see as a birthright). The only way to stop the death spiral is to kill, or drastically weaken, solar. If exploiting the race and inequality wedge is the pathway to do so, so be it.

And playbook users are brilliant at exploiting this wedge. As an opener to its NEM report, ALEC's author notes "net metering policies are *doubly regressive*, being generally available to and used by the well off, and placing additional cost burdens on the less fortunate."[43] This sincere-sounding statement belies a more sinister motive, but it is a familiar strategy. As Jacqui Patterson notes in a 2020 *New York Times* article focused on the new strategies deployed by the utility industry to turn communities of color against solar energy, Brown and Black communities are all too familiar with the system being stacked against them, so when utility company officials approach them and say something like solar is "unfair," the communities assume they are telling the truth.[44]

The goal of ALEC and utilities is to effectively limit access to solar. They have seized on a preexisting racial wedge to do so. They wish to restructure rates to make solar so expensive that it will revert back to being something only available to wealthy people, effectively guaranteeing utility control of the electricity system. And all this outcry regarding equity is happening just as innovations in technology and finance have made solar panels more accessible to low- to moderate-income utility customers either directly, through lease programs, or community solar programs (discussed in chapter 5). Moreover, this outcry is happening decades after dirty fossil fuels have scarred Black and Brown communities, limited the life outcomes of these same communities, and caused climate change catastrophes that have already, and will continue to, impact those same communities in disproportionate measure. If ALEC and the utility industry cared so deeply about equity, they would work actively to ensure that solar policies include the marginalized communities their industries have harmed.

Strategies to Advance Equity and Justice in Net Metering

Well-designed rooftop solar programs can provide much-needed benefits to low-income communities and communities of color, but they must center the needs of these communities, as well as reckon with the racist energy system of the past. As the Puerto Rico and California examples illustrate, low-income communities, elders, and the sick are the most vulnerable when a weather event strikes. It logically follows that these communities should be targeted by policies designed to provide more reliable power. Although each community, region, and state has its own complex landscape regarding vulnerability and energy burdens, this section highlights three broad key policy approaches to foreground equity in the design of NEM approaches.

Prioritize and Place a Premium on Rooftop Solar in Environmental Justice Communities

Prioritizing environmental justice communities in solar adoption can mitigate health impacts, as well as bring much-needed economic benefits to such communities. As is well documented, low-income communities pay a larger percentage of their household income to meet energy needs than those with higher incomes. This energy burden impacts several aspects of life. For example, as chronicled by Diana Hernández and as well known by low- to moderate-income households, those facing extreme energy burdens tend to make trade-offs concerning household purchases and behavior. Such trade-offs can include utilizing dangerous mechanisms to heat the home, going without air conditioning during heat waves, and simply foregoing necessary purchases like food and medicine.

Policies should prioritize implementation of rooftop solar in areas burdened by fossil fuel pollution with the goal of reducing the impacts of harmful emissions in such communities. These communities, known as environmental justice communities, tend to be poor communities, low-income communities, and communities of color that have faced disproportionate burdens under the current fossil fuel–driven centralized energy system. Where, for technical (and political) reasons, policies place limits on the overall amount of rooftop solar that may be adopted within a broader area, policy makers should prioritize and target further adoption in historically burdened communities. Whereas early adopters of solar power tended to be affluent and White, any focus on increased adoption should first focus on environmental justice communities. Policy makers could do that by implementing a rubric that takes into consideration the environmental burdens of a region and simply restrict or limit rooftop solar implementation in other, nonburdened, communities until rooftop solar penetration has reached a certain saturation point in environmental justice communities.

Regulators should also rethink value of solar propositions to increase value for rooftop solar in environmental justice communities. Doing so would incentivize solar companies to actually seek out communities of color for rooftop solar development, rather than eschewing them for more affluent communities. This type of incentive could help to overcome the implicit (and explicit) biases against working in low-income communities and communities of color. For homeowners in such communities, the increased focus on solar adoption could lead to long-term savings. For renters, landlords might have greater incentives to invest in rooftop solar panels knowing that they will receive a premium on the electricity produced. The policy would need to require that these savings be passed on to the renter to lower overall electricity bills, but the landlord could offer any excess energy back to the grid and receive the benefit. Given the history of exploitation in low-income communities and communities of color, the policy would also need to prescribe and standardize the contractual and compensation parameters to minimize the possibility of abuse.

Increase Overall Value of Solar Generally

Policy debates over the value of solar have tended to focus myopically on the value that 1 kilowatt-hour of solar energy replaces on the electric grid. For example, a utility typically purchases power from an energy market that has a mix of many possible sources of electricity (for example, oil, gas, or coal). This unit of power has a cost, called the wholesale rate. As discussed, the utility industry and fossil fuel industry proponents would like the value of solar to mirror the wholesale rate (or avoided cost). They claim that solar energy adds no more value to the grid than a normal unit of fossil fuel–derived energy would provide, but that is mistaken. Solar energy offers potential as a clean energy resource that, over a longer time horizon, diminishes health risks and reduces the overall risks associated with climate change. Policy makers have been reluctant to adopt such a long-range view, but such health and environmental risks must play into the calculus of the overall value of solar.

New York's regulators have made this shift. Its value stack for solar energy replaces NEM and is far from perfect, but the compensation rate "combines the wholesale price of energy with the distinct elements of" distributed energy resources "that benefit the grid: the avoided carbon emissions, the cost savings to customers and utilities, and other savings from avoiding expensive capital investments."[45] Advocates should fight to add these qualitative measures into the overall value of solar. Including environmental and health benefits in the overall value mix will increase the compensation rate available to rooftop solar adopters. A higher compensation rate will result in greater rooftop solar access in the communities that need it most and will ultimately reduce climate burdens for future generations.

Provide Financial and Legal Support for Intervention

A consistent theme in many regulatory proceedings involving NEM is complexity. Lack of access to closely held utility data comes in a very close second. Although some states, like California, provide financial support to parties allowed to intervene in regulatory proceedings involving utilities, the vast majority of states do not.[46] This lack of support puts would-be low-income participants at a stark disadvantage to the monied interests who owe their largesse to utility customers themselves. Even more insidious is the commitment of groups like ALEC to limit access to customer-owned and customer-sited distributed energy resources. These groups essentially serve as think tanks for the utility industry. Payment for intervenors would allow communities to hire their own experts and lawyers to engage in the often complex and document-heavy regulatory proceedings that actually structure the energy system.

Communities and advocates should fight for this type of funding and urge lawmakers to consider reallocating a portion of utility revenues for this purpose. This basic access to the regulatory process would help to ensure that the diverse voices of the most marginalized are heard in the proceedings that affect them the most.

CHAPTER 5

Community Energy:
The Devil Is in the Details

An elder in Hawaiʻi once asked me, "What is energy?" My team, a group of engaged law students at the University of Hawaiʻi, and I had just delivered a six-hour program that delved into the minutiae of Hawaiʻi energy law and policy. We started with an hour-long presentation that traced the history of the state's public utility and then divided meeting attendees—a mix of young and old people, Native Hawaiians and people of various ethnic backgrounds, and mostly low- to moderate-income residents—into small groups. We asked each group to answer questions about their highest aspirations for the utility and their vision for Hawaii's energy future.

We were quite proud of ourselves. The meeting was a part of a series of three community meetings our group would hold over a two-week period along the northern shore of Oahu, which houses 100 percent of the island's wind turbines.[1] Many of the wind turbines had been placed in the Waimea Valley, a place sacred to Native Hawaiians, as well as in close proximity to low-income communities of color. Most of the workshop attendees lived in or had some connection to the north shore of Oahu. The meetings took place within a broader regulatory drama that featured a courtship between the state's much-despised investor-owned utility, Hawaiian Electric Company (HECO), and a Florida-based utility company, NextEra Energy, concerning the purchase of HECO's assets. Many residents feared that NextEra sought to use the islands as a laboratory for energy experimentation.[2] They also worried that NextEra would use Hawai'i to show other utilities how to tamp down on consumer-owned rooftop solar, a tactic the behemoth utility had already deployed with great success in Florida (the Sunshine State), through its subsidiary, Florida Power and Light.[3] Although very few ratepayers would express love for HECO, it was the devil we knew. NextEra Energy posed a much darker threat.

My team had two reasons for organizing these meetings. On the one hand, we hoped to introduce the more technical, regulatory, and legal aspects of Hawai'i's energy system into the broader lexicon. We worked closely with community leaders to develop what we hoped was a straightforward, jargon-free presentation. On the other hand, we hoped to illuminate and tease out the true stakes of the proposed deal between HECO and NextEra while also empowering community members to envision their own energy future, free from legal, technological, or regulatory constraints. From that place of highest hopes and wildest dreams, we planned to make the case to regulators and lawmakers that they should design energy policy that mirrored community desires.

As one veteran lawyer in the energy community expressed to me, energy issues in Hawai'i, unlike many places, are discussed at the kitchen table. Hawai'i residents suffer the burden of paying high electricity costs (the highest in the United States) alongside high costs for food and housing. Although Hawai'i's volcanic land is fertile, for centuries it has been used to support the once-profitable monoculture crops of sugarcane and pineapple.[4] That means that other foods needed for daily life—vegetables, for example—need to be imported to the islands, with increased economic and environmental costs. A grassroots food justice and food security movement has begun to advocate for a sustainable food system based on locally grown, organic food that does not rely on fossil fuels; however, the multibillion-dollar fossil fuel–based tourism industry requires the constant shipping of food to the islands to quell the hunger tourists face after hours spent lounging on Hawai'i's beaches. Early on in my time in the state, I heard that the food insecurity is so acute that, at any given time, the islands only have forty-eight hours' worth of food, a possibility that chilled me to my core. In reality, the amount of time may be closer to ten days, but that is no less comforting.[5]

On the energy side, oil and gas are not endogenous (local) to the islands. They, too, must be imported in, at cost, even though Hawaii's landscape is one of the richest in the world for clean and renewable energy resources. During the day, the sun shines somewhere on the islands. The Pacific blue waves lap the shorelines with a predictable frequency. The trade winds blow at a (mostly) regular pattern across the islands. Water flows from the top of Hawai'i's peaks through freshwater tributaries that eventually reach the sea. And geothermal energy, the powerful source of clean energy that comes from deep within Earth's core, lies just below the Earth's surface.

Despite fertile land and abundant energy resources, the costs of food and energy remain exorbitant. Many often joke that this is "the cost of paradise," but the deeper, often unspoken, sentiment is that powerful interests, including the electric utility, have a lock on the resources in the state, and these interests have systematically extracted wealth from the poorest, most rural, and brownest communities across the archipelago. Our community meetings, held in a mix of rural and low-income communities where wealthy surf pros routinely brush shoulders with third- and fourth-generation farmers, took place within this complex landscape, where the mark of colonialism sounded less like an echo and more like a scream.

The fundamental flaw of the meetings (which, I'll admit, I designed) was to presume a common understanding of the question, what is energy? The answer, of course, informs our understanding of how we organize our systems to provide access to natural resources. If we believe that we, in fact, *are* energy and that energy also means food, water, air, and sunlight—the things we and most living beings on this planet need to thrive—we design systems that provide a harmonious connection to energy. Rather than "harnessing" power, we flow with it. If, on the other hand, we believe that energy exists separate and apart from us, we design legal systems that erect barriers to accessing vital, life sustaining energy. We commodify it.

The Native Hawaiians understood this complexity. Their cosmology, or worldview, recognizes humans as only one part of a complex ecosystem, of which we are stewards, but over which we hold no dominion. In the Native Hawaiian cosmology, the fish and plants that sustained the Native Hawaiians were also relatives and ancestors.[6] The precolonial Hawaiian system of land and resource management, the ahupua'a system, seemed to reflect this understanding of our role to protect the ecosystem as well as honor it as a vital part of us. The ahupua'a system segmented each island into pie-shaped wedges. In general, to maximize the diversity of resources in each segment, Hawaiians divided the land from ocean to mountaintop.[7] The fattest part of the wedge started at the ocean and became narrower as the wedge sliced up the mountainous part of each island (the Hawaiian archipelago benefits from fairly uniform geography across the islands, forged by volcanoes). Each slice contained the vital resources to sustain the beings within it, starting from the ocean and the many resources it contained, to the freshwater sheds created by the rivers flowing downhill, to the plants and animals that thrive within the watershed. For example, terrestrial zone designations included wet forest, remote forest, agroforest, and habitation zones.[8]

A ruler managed the ahupuaʻa and the people within his kuleana, a Hawaiian word that means privilege and responsibility.

If sustainability had a poster child, this would be it. For example, the Hawaiians prohibited fishing during spawning season.[9] They also created shoreline and inland fishponds ("loko iʻa") known as among the most sophisticated in the Pacific. The fishponds not only allowed diverse species of fish to thrive, but provided a sustainably raised food source. Pond managers created a system of walls and gates that allowed smaller fish to swim freely into the pond, but as fish got bigger, they became trapped in the pond.[10] According to one study, at one point, nearly four hundred fishponds functioned across the main Hawaiian islands and offered a sustainable food source to the nearly one-million-strong island population.[11] In contrast, nearly all the fishponds in the archipelago have disappeared, and the nearly 1.4 million people in the current population must rely on imported food to survive.[12]

I believe the elder's question stemmed from this rich history and connection to the planet and the life-sustaining resources on it. With one question, she illuminated the hubris of US energy policy: we cannot purport to control or sell that which belongs to all of us. Our entire system of energy law is designed to support that assumption. Unbeknownst to me, I had designed the meeting with the invisible baggage of colonization and a Western view of energy. In my ignorance, I had structured the meeting to preclude more creative possibilities for the energy future. I left chastened, but with a more expansive view of the potential of our energy system.

What Is Community Energy?

Community energy programs aim to remedy the underlying flaws within the current model of energy access by creating pathways for communities to develop, own, and manage their own energy resources. The programs emerged as a response to the net energy metering programs discussed in chapter 4. Although net energy metering allows individual homeowners and business owners to generate and sell electricity from their rooftops, the programs generally leave out large portions of the population. Renters, apartment and condominium dwellers, those with shaded rooftops, and low- to moderate-income community members often cannot benefit from net energy metering programs.[13] Community energy programs emerged as a response to this gap in access to locally managed clean energy.

Community energy means something different in each of the twenty-three states that have adopted a community energy policy.[14] See figure 5-1.

Figure 5-1. States That Have Adopted Community Solar Policies

Source: NC Clean Energy Technology Center, "The 50 States of Solar: 2019 Policy Review and Q4 Quarterly Report," January 2020.

Community energy also has a different meaning depending on who is speaking. For most energy democracy advocates, community energy means small-scale energy production located within a community, controlled by the community, and owned by the community. As authors of the "Solar with Justice" guide to community solar state, community groups in "under-resourced communities and environmental justice organizations . . . seek to advance solar projects that are located in the community, are shaped by the community, and provide tangible benefits to the community, including *local wealth building*."[15]

The scale of the energy matters. Small-scale energy avoids many of the impacts associated with large-scale energy facilities, which tend to disproportionately burden low-income communities of color and rural communities. Community control matters, too. When communities control their own power, they can determine where a project is located, how the energy is distributed, and which areas of the community (for example, health care centers, community centers, schools, and low-income housing) should be prioritized in terms of energy access. Ownership also matters and maximizes the economic benefits that flow from the project to the community through lower bills or even subsidized rates for vulnerable community members.

By contrast, when the "solar industry and utilities use the term 'community solar,' they generally refer to a large shared installation in which customers can purchase subscriptions or ownership of part of the" solar project.[16] For developers and utilities, the "installation does not necessarily have to be in the same community as the subscribers and can often be located elsewhere in an electric utility's service territory."[17] Further, a shared solar installation is typically owned and controlled by a developer, rather than the community.

Because the term *community energy* can refer to such a range of project types, advocates should ensure that language concerning community energy is clear and advances some key principles. In theory, community energy programs would allow for communities to be able to control and manage energy resources, namely solar energy. Like net energy metering, community energy programs would offer program participants the chance to receive a one-for-one bill credit from the energy they produce. In an ideal world, community energy programs would also target low- to moderate-income utility customers to give them the opportunity to reap economic benefits from a community-scale energy project. Community energy programs would also manage controversial issues like the size and location of energy facilities by incentivizing the development of locally sited, community-scale energy projects.

Community energy policies gained traction because of the potential to realize all the foregoing ambitions, but the myriad programs under development around the United States stray far from these original promises. The result is a patchwork of methods and approaches that have largely replicated the inequalities of the investor-owned energy development approach. The following section describes in greater detail these design flaws.

Challenges with Hawai'i's Community-Based Renewable Energy Program

In the spring of 2015, just a year after the now-infamous Order and Inclinations and the same time the state adopted its ambitious 100 percent renewable energy goal, state lawmakers passed Hawai'i's community energy legislation, Act 100; later that summer, the governor signed the legislation into law. At the time, Hawai'i had the highest per capita adoption of rooftop solar in the United States, at 17 percent, but only homeowners and business owners could avail themselves of rooftop solar.[18] Legislators designed the community energy law to address the dearth of opportunities for low- to moderate-income Hawaiians and condominium dwellers to participate in the generation of clean energy and the economic benefits that came along with it.

The language of the statute offers some insight into the underlying issues the legislation hoped to resolve:

> The legislature finds that all Hawai'i residents should be able to participate in and enjoy the economic, environmental, and societal benefits of renewable energy. Spurred by the Hawai'i clean energy initiative and increasingly affordable clean energy options, such as solar photovoltaic systems, localized renewable energy generation technology has become increasingly attainable.
>
> While residential solar energy use has grown dramatically across the State in recent years, many residents and businesses are currently unable to directly participate in renewable energy generation because of their location, building type, access to the electric utility grid, and other impediments. The community-based renewable energy program seeks to rectify this inequity by dramatically expanding the market for eligible renewable energy resources to include residential and business renters, occupants of residential and commercial buildings with shaded or improperly oriented roofs, and other groups who are unable to access the benefits of onsite clean energy generation.[19]

The community energy ideals discussed—locally owned, locally sited, and locally managed community-scale energy projects—framed the lead-up to Hawai'i's decision to adopt a community energy law and policy. In Hawai'i, a community energy policy could link back to the ahupua'a system of natural resource management. The policy could reflect the Hawaiian ideal of kuleana, or responsibility, for shepherding natural resources. Moreover, within the policy, energy itself could be treated more like something to be managed as a common-held good, rather than a commodity to be exploited by powerful corporate interests. Hawai'i's resulting policy framework fell far short of these possibilities.

The statute makes clear that *any* person may own or operate a community-based renewable energy project, as long as that person complies with law. The law also calls on the state's utilities to design a community energy program with the oversight of the state energy regulator, the Public Utilities Commission (PUC). As one would suspect, the investor-owned utility's early program designs were very complex and clearly self-beneficial. Solar and environmental advocates formed a separate stakeholder group to develop an alternative policy. I listened in on several meetings of this group, which eventually coalesced around a set of ideas regarding what the community solar policy should provide. Their ideas influenced the policy ultimately accepted by the PUC, but also reflected the biases of the participants that created it.

For example, although the legislature passed the community energy policy in explicit recognition that prior distributed energy generation programs had excluded low- to moderate-income utility customers, solar and environmental stakeholders expressed reluctance to include provisions that focused on this group of customers. In fact, when I raised the issue of low- to moderate-income ratepayer access to community solar in a stakeholder meeting, participants brushed my concerns aside, reasoning that regulators would struggle so much with HECO's community energy framework that issues of social and racial equity would need to be dealt with after establishing the basic outline of the program. They worried that a focus on equity would derail the entire process, a perspective akin to the climate change fundamentalism outlined in chapter 3.

After two years of a complex regulatory proceeding, the PUC adopted a final version of the program in December 2017. It took another seven months for the PUC to approve HECO's final documentation in connection with the program. Although policy makers could have adopted a community energy policy that required the creation of locally sited energy that prioritized benefits to low- to moderate-income customers, they did not.

Hawai'i's community-based renewable energy program is complex and involves multiple phases of implementation. Under Hawai'i's community-based renewable energy program adopted by the PUC, a developer (subscriber organization) initiates a project and pays a one-time $1,000 fee to the utility (the administrator) to get the project off the ground. A subscriber organization may be any type of business entity or a nonprofit organization, but business entities are the only entities able to take advantage of the federal investment tax credit that offsets the overall costs of the investment.[20] The subscriber organization is responsible for leasing or purchasing land for the project, as well as securing community members or participants for the project. Through a subscription agreement, the participants (subscribers) sign up to receive an amount of energy produced by the energy project, and pay a program fee determined by the developer to participate in the program.[21]

For the first phase of Hawai'i's program, the credit rate, or amount that the subscriber organization receives for the energy it produces, ranges from fifteen cents per kilowatt-hour to twenty-six cents per kilowatt-hour, depending on the island where the project is located. In 2018, residential electricity prices on the islands ranged from thirty-one cents per kilowatt-hour to forty cents per kilowatt-hour. The fifteen to twenty-six cent credit rate amounts to around half of what early rooftop solar customers received for the energy they produced. This inequity matters. It means that subscriber organizations participating in the program are incentivized to develop larger projects to capture the benefits of economy of scale of a larger energy facility. A larger facility means that the developer saves on building costs and recovers more costs when it provides electricity to customers. In this way, the project looks less like a "community energy project" and more like a large, utility-scale energy project. The low compensation rate provided to subscriber organizations also means that community solar customers will receive a lower reduction on their utility bills than early adopters of rooftop solar received because the subscriber organization can only pass on the amount of savings that allows it to recoup its investment in the project. This structure forecloses opportunities for community-scale development and also disincentivizes participation by low- to moderate-income rate utility customers, who are less likely to take on the risk, cost, and complexity of a subscription.

Finally, the program does not focus on or prioritize opportunities for low- to moderate-income ratepayers in any significant way, but notes that in the second phase of the program, if the utility wishes to participate in the community energy program, half of its subscribers must be low- to moderate-income customers. This design element is notable because it forces the utility to use its resources creatively. It also recognizes that the utility is uniquely positioned to assist low- to moderate-income customers. It comes too late in the implementation of the overall community-based renewable energy program, however, and allows subscriber organizations to avoid targeting low- to moderate-income ratepayers as they develop projects.

The cost and scale aspects of Hawai'i's policy design trace back to the entities that played the largest roles in the regulatory process that led to the creation of Hawai'i's community-based renewable energy program. As the filings of the various parties in the regulatory proceeding reflect, the utility aimed to make Hawai'i's community-based energy program so cost prohibitive that it would be unattractive to solar developers interested in developing community energy projects. The utility offered an exchange rate for energy produced that was so low that the solar industry responded with indignation. The solar industry, on the other hand, had little interest in getting low- to moderate-income ratepayers to actually participate in the program and instead wanted to create a program for those middle- to high-income utility customers who lived in communities that were unsuitable for rooftop solar. For the solar industry, the sweet spot would be moderately sized energy projects that were located away from communities, but that offered the solar company similar payback advantages of rooftop solar. Under this model, project participants would receive a slight discount on their electricity bill, and solar companies would reap the lion's share of economic benefits.

Advocates—typically environmentalists intent on seeing more clean energy on the electricity grid—like to shape the struggle as one between the utility and the solar industry. This framing belies a deeper conflict, one between large, corporate interests and low- to moderate-income people. In the energy transition, low- to moderate-income communities are now fighting both utilities and solar companies to gain fair access to resources that belong to us all. Although the solar industry emerged from Hawaiʻi's community energy battle with a larger slice of the pie than the utility would have liked, the most vulnerable communities in Hawaiʻi ultimately lost. Hawaiʻi's first year in its community-based renewable energy program reflects this loss. In the summer of 2019, an independent observer appointed by the PUC noted a "material rate of failure to date" of submitted project applications, limited outreach, and lack of community group participation in the information sessions related to the program.[22]

Mililani Tech Solar I, the first community solar project approved by the utility, further illustrates the limitations of the PUC-approved community energy model. The project, approved in September 2019, includes 864 solar panels located in an Oahu community named Mililani. In many ways, Mililani's residents mirror the ethnic diversity of Honolulu County. The community is 17.5 percent White, compared with 21.7 percent in the county; 1.7 percent Black (2.8 percent in the county); 42.4 percent Asian (43 percent in the county); 33.1 percent mixed race (22.6 percent in the county); and 11.7 percent Hispanic/Latinx (10 percent in the county). Of the 8,800 households, nearly 75 percent of the residents in the community own their own homes, with an average home value of $620,200. With a median income of $95,481, the community is slightly wealthier than the county overall, where the mean income was around $83,000 in 2018. On the whole, the project serves a racially and ethnically diverse community (like many in Hawai'i), but the community largely comprises middle-class homeowners who, arguably, could benefit from the state's rooftop solar programs anyway. Although the Mililani project marks a significant success for the program, it falls far short of reaching the types of communities who have been the most burdened by Hawai'i's fossil fuel energy system. It also foreshadows the ways that the most vulnerable communities will likely continue to be left out of the clean energy transition in meaningful ways.

Oahu's Waianae community might have been a better place to locate the island's first community energy project. The community houses or is in close proximity to *all* the island's dirty generation, a wastewater treatment facility, and landfills.[23] The geography on the west side of the island also makes solar energy particularly attractive. In fact, one developer, AES Solar West Oahu, has been approved to develop a utility-scale 12.5-megawatt solar project that includes a significant storage component in the area. With its significant environmental burdens; relatively low-income (median $59,000 income), significant Native Hawaiian (38 percent), Latinx (20.8), and mixed-race (40 percent) population; and prime solar real estate, regulators and the utility should have prioritized community solar development in this community. The structure of the existing community-based renewable energy policy, which limits the reimbursement rate for energy produced and does not create specific requirements for low- to moderate-income participation in the program, all but guarantees that middle-class communities will continue to be the primary beneficiaries of Hawaiʻi's community-based renewable energy transition.

How Did We Get Here?

It would be easy to blame the utilities and the solar industry for excluding actual communities from the design of community energy policy, but the problem may have originated with the US Department of Energy (DOE). In 2012, the DOE released a playbook of its own to guide the approach to community energy around the United States. The guide stemmed from the Sunshot Initiative, an effort by the federal government to bring as much solar energy on the US energy grid as possible. Looking back, it sounds like such a quaint effort considering that the federal government under the Trump administration is doing all it can to actively limit opportunities for clean energy growth. The devil of the Sunshot Initiative is really in the details, however.

The DOE's seventy-six-page guide spawned an entire field of community energy policies and model policies that focus on three particular types of community solar policy:

1. **Utility-sponsored model:** The utility will own and operate the project, which is open to voluntary customer participation.
2. **Special purpose entity model:** Individuals join a business enterprise, which develops the community energy project.
3. **Nonprofit model:** A nonprofit organization administers the community energy project on behalf of donors or other stakeholders.[24]

In all three models, a solar generation facility is constructed; a promoter, or sponsor, solicits subscriptions for the project; and once the project is fully subscribed, the promoter receives relevant tax or renewable energy credits and the electricity generated is credited to subscribers.

The predominant models advanced by the National Renewable Energy Laboratory remove the locus of control for generation away from the consumer, focus on utility-scale generation and economies of scale, and do little to foster more distributed models of generation. A cottage industry of sorts has emerged to capitalize on new models of community solar generation, but DOE emphasizes that utilities should take the lead in developing such projects. In many ways, the community-shared solar model is more of the same approach to development, but by a different name.[25]

By promoting community energy models in such a way, the DOE effectively limits opportunities to conceptualize the energy system consistent with principles of actual democratic ownership and control. Moreover, the DOE's model fails to center the concerns of those who stand to benefit the most from community-based clean energy: marginalized communities historically impacted by fossil fuel development. In fact, the policy guide does more to buttress the utility industry—by making utilities central players in the community energy design—and the solar industry, who are the "developers" behind the program structure. This design not only leaves actual communities out of central roles in the program, but leaves the most powerful players within the energy landscape to haggle along the margins of price and size. When community energy policy emerged on the policy scene on the heels of the rapid adoption of rooftop solar, policy makers understandably needed examples and models for community energy design, but the ubiquity of the DOE's model is nonetheless disappointing.

As noted, twenty-three states and the District of Columbia have adopted some sort of community energy policy (see figure 5-1). Despite the DOE model's design flaws, research conducted by the North Carolina Clean Energy Technology Center indicates that some states have also made attempts to include provisions for low- to moderate-income ratepayers (table 5-1).

Table 5-1. State Low-Income Provisions

California	The CPUC directed Pacific Gas & Electric and Southern California Edison to solicit Community Solar Green Tariff projects to serve disadvantaged communities in the San Joaquin Valley.
Connecticut	Connecticut's shared clean energy facility program rules reserve 20 percent of project capacity for low-income customers.
Illinois	The Illinois Solar for All program includes an additional six to thirteen cents per kilowatt-hour for low-income community solar projects.
Maryland	Maryland's pilot program includes a 60-megawatt carve-out for projects focused on low- to moderate-income customers.
Massachusetts	The SMART program includes an adder of six cents per kilowatt-hour for community solar projects serving low- to moderate-income customers.
New Hampshire	Low- and moderate-income community solar projects are eligible for a three cents per kilowatt-hour credit adder.
New Jersey	New Jersey's community solar pilot program rules include a 40 percent carve-out for low- to moderate-income customers.
Oregon	Oregon's community solar rules include a 10 percent carve-out and 20 percent subscription discount for income-qualified customers.

Source: North Carolina Clean Energy Technology Center, 50 States of Solar, 2019 Policy Review and Q4 Quarterly Report.

Many other policies, however, suffer from the same flaws that plagued Hawai'i's policy design:

1. They are premium products that offer little benefit for low- to moderate-income utility customers because they create barriers to entry or provide too few economic benefits to participants.
2. They offer no actual benefits of local ownership and control.

3. They mask what is ultimately a wealth transfer from the utility industry and taxpayers to the solar industry.

These policies simply reinforce the existing power structure. They leave communities whose lives have been shaped by the fossil fuel system behind in the energy transition when, in fact, they should be at the front of the line to receive the new system's benefits. This lack of imagination should not limit possibilities to realize truly equitable community energy policy.

How to Create Equitable and Just Community Energy Policy

Community energy projects, often in the form of community solar, fundamentally implicate a community's relationship to energy. If well designed, community energy policies offer communities the ability to control, own, and manage their own energy resources, as well as receive much-needed economic benefits from them. Although places like Samsø island in Denmark have illustrated that community-owned energy can be large in scale and supply the energy needs beyond those of the owners, community energy can also be local and offer critical backup support. Community energy holds this promise, but because those at the design table often advance the interests of the incumbent utility or the solar industry, communities get left out.

We desperately need more research on the several dozen community energy projects that currently exist in the United States to determine what actually works for marginalized communities and which model offers true economic and ownership benefits. One state, Minnesota, however, is consistently referenced as a success when it comes to community energy. According to John Farrell at the Institute for Local Self-Reliance, policy design accounts for much of Minnesota's community energy success.[26] Unlike Hawai'i and other states, the program has no caps on the development of community solar projects. Instead, with a maximum project size, the policy emphasizes small-scale development. On the compensation side, the utility must purchase all the energy produced by the project, and project subscribers receive the full retail rate for energy their share of the project produces, including for any excess generation, which also differs from the Hawai'i program design.

The community energy movement is already under way around the United States, and although many attempts have been made to effectively design and implement community energy policies, it is not the end of the story. Advocates and policy makers still have the opportunity to create policies that center equity and place the needs, hopes, and dreams of those who have been the most burdened by the current energy system at the front of the line to receive the benefits of the clean energy system. Advocates must press for a new vision for community energy, rooted in ideals of energy as something that belongs to all of us, and for our collective benefit. Community energy policies should include, at a minimum, the following features.

Emphasize the inclusion of low- to moderate-income stakeholders at the policy design table. Stakeholders influence program and policy design. Community energy regulatory proceedings serve as a key battlefront in the clean energy transition. It's where policy makers allocate the benefits and burdens of clean energy development and where the rules of the game are established. Community stakeholders and advocates representing marginalized ratepayers must be at the table to ensure vital carve-outs for frontline communities. Their presence is also vital to ensure that community energy policy offers real opportunities for community ownership of community energy projects. In Hawai'i's community-based renewable energy proceeding, communities lacked a voice. Although the environmental community and solar industry were well represented in the stakeholder group formed to counter the utility's models for the community energy program, all acquiesced to a policy design that ultimately left marginalized communities out.

Emphasize economic participation and ownership by low- to moderate-income customers. Participation in the design of community energy projects does not go far enough to guarantee authentic participation in community energy projects. Community solar advocates have defined participation as providing economic "adders" for projects that include a certain percentage of low- to moderate-income subscribers or increase the compensation rate available in projects serving certain communities.[27] But adders do not go far enough. Actual participation requires the economic participation in projects in the form of co-ownership of projects. Incorporating co-ownership into the design of community solar policy will require that third-party developers partner with community organizations and community members in the development of projects early in the development process. Community energy policies can include this requirement, and community advocates should demand it.

Emphasize community-scale development. Community-scale energy projects (particularly when paired with storage) can offer communities vital energy when major climate events impact the centralized grid. They can be designed to offer power to the adjacent community and to support critical community infrastructure, such as hospitals, community centers, and schools. Community energy policy offers an opportunity to mitigate community vulnerability, as long as such policies are designed to privilege small-scale projects and work to include a storage component.

Emphasize community-sited energy projects. Community-sited development offers similar, climate-related benefits to community-scale energy projects. It also offers the benefit of minimizing the impact of fossil fuel generation in burdened communities. "Peaker plants" are facilities that are used at high-peak times and tend to be located in low-income Black and Brown communities. Siting community energy in these communities could help to mitigate the impact of peaker facilities; at the proper scale, siting community energy projects that include battery storage could be a game changer in such communities. Community energy policy design should prioritize such development by creating incentives for developers who seek to locate projects within proximity to fossil fuel generation and peaker facilities.

Emphasize providing the retail-rate exchange for energy produced by the project. Policies should offer the retail rate of exchange as a reflection of the true value of community-sized projects. The rate of exchange for the energy produced impacts every aspect of the project. It impacts whether a developer can afford to develop the project because of how much the developer can sell the project's energy to the grid. The exchange, or credit, rate also impacts whether ratepayers view participation in the project as an expense or a benefit, given the documentation and sub-scription fees often associated with community energy projects. Finally, the credit rate matters due to equity. Early solar adopters tended to be affluent and White. Legislators and advocates have turned to commu-nity energy as a possible way to bridge the access gap between those who have access to solar and those who do not. Lowering the exchange rate just as solar becomes available to low-income communities and com-munities of color is akin to changing the rules of the game right before the final quarter. It's patently unfair, and regulators, lawmakers, and stakeholders must remain cognizant of this deep inequity.

So, what *is* energy? Based on my time in Hawai'i, I know that energy is much more than something that exists outside of us. It flows within and between us, and it also *belongs* to all of us. Community energy holds promise as a policy tool and a mechanism to lift folks out of poverty and reduce energy burden. We must remain vigilant, however, and ensure that the "energy as commodity" model does not shut out opportunities for collective ownership and management of a resource that exists for our common benefit.

CHAPTER 6

Access to Capital: A Way to End Solar Segregation

When I was growing up, some nights I watched my mom sit at our kitchen table with a thick legal notebook. It might be a payday, or maybe the middle of the week, but it was always in the evening, always after dinner. She filled the college-ruled lines with her tiny, neat script, listing all our monthly household expenses on one side of the ledger and the amounts on the other. She wrote in pencil because she knew she would have to shuffle some of our monthly bills around in order to pay them. As she often said, on a monthly basis, she would have to "borrow from Peter to pay Paul." She always prioritized the basics: rent, food, and the light bill. But there was never enough. Her limited salary as a government worker disqualified our family of three for any meaningful public assistance, but it was far from sufficient to keep our household afloat.

I remember some of the coldest nights in our small apartment in Austin. On those nights, we huddled around the oven to warm our bones before bed. Sometimes we ran out of hot water, and my mom used the stove top to boil hot water and add it to our baths. I remember submerging myself in lukewarm water, scrubbing my body through chattering teeth. At night, we piled blankets on our bed, and we always wore layers to stay warm in a home where my sister and I were under strict orders to keep the thermostat at sixty to sixty-five degrees. These habits followed me to Boston, where my then-partner and I, both law students, kept our home just warm enough to avoid freezing the pipes. We didn't know that it was unusual until an overnight guest commented on how cold and uncomfortable our house was.

I thought that I might share someone else's story and experience around energy insecurity, but these images flooded in. Like many of the people who struggle with energy poverty (lack of access to energy) and energy insecurity (lack of ability to pay for energy), I felt intense shame in recalling the ways my low-income family struggled to pay the bills, to keep ourselves warm, and to feel comfortable in our home at night. Looking back, I realize how much precarity pervaded my young mother's day-to-day life. As a single mother of two growing girls and the primary source of income for our family, my mom held the sole responsibility for our food, shelter, and day-to-day needs. At any moment, if her calculations of which bills would clear on which date were wrong, we might have the lights turned out, we might not have adequate food for the week, or, in the worst cases, we might need to move. Growing up, I experienced all this instability, but—thankfully—I carried little of the constant stress associated with it.

In conducting research for this book, I realized our family was far from alone. In the United States, a place with abundant wealth and seemingly infinite financial resources, families lack access to a safety net sufficient to offer true security and stability when it comes to energy. Energy poverty refers to the lack of access to life-sustaining energy.[1] When folks imagine energy poverty, they frequently think of people in faraway places, like Sub-Saharan Africa and Asia;[2] according to recent studies, however, many Americans also experience issues around energy access.[3]

Experts recognize that households should spend around 6 percent on energy needs for that energy to be affordable.[4] Low-income households routinely incur an energy burden that far exceeds this amount. In many communities, low-income households pay more than 20 percent of average household income to meet their energy needs. According to one researcher, the poorest Americans, at below 50 percent of the poverty line, experience extreme energy burdens. These families spend around 35 percent of their income to pay their energy bills.[5] This disparity exists in my home state of Texas, where these days the average electricity rates hover around 8.5 cents per kilowatt hour, around four cents cheaper than the national average. According to a recent study on the home energy affordability gap, in that state the "number of households facing unaffordable home energy burdens is staggering." Further, in Texas, low-income households with incomes under 50 percent of the federal poverty level pay around 29 percent of their annual income to energy bills. Those at 50 to 100 percent of the poverty line face a 16 percent energy burden.[6] All this is in a state where energy is relatively cheap. Although I grew up in the 1980s, these data begin to explain the extreme struggle my mother faced to keep our household afloat.

The federal government has developed national programs to address energy poverty. LIHEAP, the Low-Income Home Energy Assistance Program, aims to fill some of these gaps by offering financial assistance to families struggling to pay their bills.[7] By many measures though, LIHEAP fails to reach the majority of those who need it[8] due to a lack of appropriate outreach[9] and a lack of adequate program funding.[10]

Some local laws also prevent electricity shutoffs for nonpaying utility customers during the winter, which offers some measure of stability to residents during the coldest months of the year.[11] Heads of these families likely shuffle around their bills to make ends meet just like my mom did, but that only allows for modest breathing room. At the end of the winter season, they face crippling energy arrears that ultimately lead to electricity shutoff anyway.[12] Moreover, some cutoff laws only protect against extreme cold.[13] Most communities lack legal protection from cutoffs in the face of the extreme heat waves now commonplace during the summer months.[14] As recent studies show, these heat waves disproportionately impact Black and Brown communities, which tend to lack green space and trees for cooling.[15]

Finally, some point to energy efficiency programs as a mechanism to assist with reducing the overall bills customers pay. These programs sound promising, too, but renters must get landlord permission to participate in home modification programs, and landlords generally have little incentive to reduce their tenants' electricity bills. Further, the homes of many low-income homeowners do not meet the basic requirements to even qualify for energy efficiency programs.[16] Such problems run the gamut, from structural to electrical wiring.[17] Most programs expect low-income customers to fix these issues before they can avail themselves of programs that might significantly reduce their energy bills.[18]

We should not forget that the burdens faced by these households are two-fold. On the one hand, low-income households pay more of overall income to meet basic household energy needs. On the other, the same households bear the burden of housing dirty, fossil fuel generation, and other electricity infrastructure, such as high-voltage transmission lines. Such is the deep irony of the design of our energy system. The poorest and most environmentally burdened yield no benefit from the very system they unwillingly and disproportionately subsidize.

Amid all these barriers and burdens for low-income families, the energy system is transforming. As discussed in chapters 4 and 5, policy changes have emerged to provide individual homeowners and communities economic benefits for self-generation (rooftop solar) and participation in community energy projects. Unfortunately, to date, only the wealthiest and whitest Americans have benefited from these policy innovations. Participation in clean energy production could not only drastically reduce energy burdens and offer a pathway to economic justice, but also lessen the impacts of fossil fuel generation.

A lack of access to credit and resources to finance clean, local energy poses the most significant barrier to low-income participation in the energy transition. These access issues not only stem from the legacy of redlining and racist perceptions of creditworthiness, but also from tax incentive programs that privilege the wealthy. The energy transition threatens to further cement the legacy of racist economic exclusion in the United States by creating veritable green zones separated by invisible, yet palpable, barriers.[19]

In light of these challenges, it might seem like a leap for low-income communities to move from energy burdens and energy insecurity to participation in the solar transition. But focusing on the deficits facing communities misses the broader, more transformative, opportunity for true economic and social empowerment available through rooftop solar access and community energy programs. It is precisely the communities filled with families like my own—single-parent households, families making too much to qualify for federal or state public assistance but making too little to thrive, and those facing extraordinary energy burdens—who stand to gain the most with this energy transition. Unfortunately, the financial tools created to allow for their participation in clean energy fall far short of the ideal.

Barriers to Accessing Capital

Investment Tax Credits and Tax Appetite

The incentives created to facilitate clean energy development erect structural barriers to the inclusion of low-income families and communities in the clean energy transition. As discussed in chapter 4, lawmakers created the investment tax credit to attract participation in solar and wind investment. The federal investment tax credit, however, incentivizes only those with sufficiently high incomes to participate in clean energy development.[20] The DOE refers to this income threshold as "tax appetite."[21] The higher an individual or business income, the more tax appetite the individual or business has. This design prevents low-income individuals and nonprofit organizations from participating in clean energy development. It also forces those who want to participate in the renewable energy transition to partner with wealthy third parties in order to realize energy projects.

When communities or individuals partner with third parties, the economic benefits flow to the community or organization through a fixed rate for energy set by the third-party partner. Under this type of scenario, the majority of the economic benefits flow to the third-party partner. As discussed in chapter 5, the community or organization will typically lack an ownership interest in the project and retain very little control over the actual project. This structure makes it difficult for communities to use clean energy development as a mechanism to advance equity and economic justice. In fact, it increases the chances that the project will actually replicate inequality, because the local community will have very little say in shaping it.

At a household level, the situation is slightly different. A family must seek out a solar partner that is willing and able to finance the family's access to solar in exchange for receiving the tax credits. Like any business, solar companies seek to minimize their business risk. Companies typically aim for middle-class customers who may lack resources or desire to pay for their solar systems outright, but who meet a threshold credit score requirement to partner with the company. This model, too, can unwittingly replicate inequality by limiting pathways for low- to moderate-income participation in clean energy investment.

Federal and state incentives have facilitated the growth and development of a thriving solar industry, but they have also facilitated a massive wealth transfer from taxpayers to the solar industry, bypassing low- to moderate-income families and communities. Moreover, the incentives have created structural barriers to inclusion in the clean energy transition, leading to what I call solar segregation.

When community energy projects involve a nonprofit or community organization and individual solar installation, companies focus on risk mitigation. Having picked the lowest hanging fruit of prosperous households, solar companies have no real incentive to engage with low- to moderate-income utility customers. Further, even when low- to moderate-income customers are involved, they reap few of the actual economic benefits of the clean energy itself. Whether intentional or not, by design, the relationship between customer and solar company structurally excludes the communities that most need clean, local energy. Solar policy design facilitates this exclusion.

Lack of Access to Meaningful Credit

Credit scores create a significant barrier to participation to solar programs. Solar panels cost money, and although the solar industry has evolved to offer loans, leases, and other financial instruments to credit-worthy homeowners and businesses, the industry does not view low-income communities as attractive partners in the renewable energy transition. The constant bill shuffling that many low-income families engage in to keep the lights on can impact their credit score, also known as the FICO score, which has become the gold standard that banks use to offer access loans. A missed or late bill can lead to a cascade of financial issues, including a declaration of bankruptcy, when a family has decided that they have no way to meet current debt obligations. The cost of energy lies at the root of many of these issues. Unfortunately, those who most need the financial instruments that can actually drive down the cost of energy and allow for true economic empowerment lack access.

Green Banks: A Mix of Successes and Failures

Green banks have emerged to fill the gaps in low- to moderate-income access to financing for rooftop solar and community energy programs. Well-known programs include the Connecticut Green Bank and the New York Green Bank. Legislatures created these programs to allow those without access to traditional financing to obtain badly needed low-interest loans to finance clean energy projects. In terms of transforming the lived experiences of low- to moderate-income communities, the results have been somewhat mixed. The good news is that the most successful banks have increased the penetration of clean energy in low- to moderate-income communities. Although this progress is laudable, the biggest economic benefits have continued to flow to solar companies. In addition, the banks and solar companies participating in bank-funded incentive programs continue to rely on credit scores to grant access to funds, further limiting the widespread availability of clean energy projects.

The Connecticut Green Bank

Industry observers hold out the Connecticut Green Bank as an exemplar of moving the needle on green finance, particularly in low- to moderate-income communities of color. Established in 2011 by the Connecticut Governor and the State's General Assembly, it was the country's first state-level green bank. The idea grew out of an idea hatched by a Yale University professor and lawmakers interested in increasing clean energy access in the state. The enacting legislation established the bank as a "quasi-public agency" superseding the Connecticut Clean Energy Fund.[22] Further, lawmakers designed the bank to use "limited public dollars to attract private capital investments."[23] The idea was that the bank would create programs to offer low-interest funding for clean energy projects, with an emphasis on rooftop solar. The bank receives the bulk of its funding through a surcharge on utility customer bills (on average, $7 to $10 per household per year). The bank also occasionally issues "green bonds" for additional revenue and owns the rights to tradeable renewable energy credits generated by the residential and commercial renewable energy projects it finances. A recent financial statement lays out the four goals of the Connecticut Green Bank as follows:

1. Attract and deploy private capital investment to finance the clean energy policy goals for Connecticut.
2. Leverage limited public funds to attract multiples of private capital investment while returning and reinvesting public funds in clean energy deployment over time.
3. Develop and implement strategies that bring down the cost of clean energy in order to make it more accessible and affordable to customers.
4. Support affordable and healthy buildings in low- to moderate-income and distressed communities by reducing the energy burden and addressing health and safety issues in their homes, business, and institutions.[24]

The Connecticut Green Bank has two units. One unit is responsible for administering incentive programs designated by state officials and ensuring that such programs are cost recoverable. The other unit focuses on providing loans to finance clean energy projects. The Residential Solar Investment Program (RSIP) incentive program offers rebates and performance-based incentives to owner-occupied residential solar installations. In its January 2019 report to the Connecticut General Assembly, the bank reported that 26 percent of the total approved projects under the program were homeowner owned projects and 74 percent were third-party owned.[25] The Solar Home Renewable Energy Credit program allows the bank "to recover its costs for administering the RSIP by selling renewable energy credits to utility companies to help the companies with compliance under the state's renewable portfolio standard."[26]

In 2015, the Green Bank established two unique incentive programs targeting low- to moderate-income participants. Each program is designed to attract solar companies to low- to moderate-income communities by increasing the amount per kilowatt-hour the companies receive for projects installed in the target communities.[27]

In general, the economic benefits offered for projects developed in low- to moderate-income communities flow to solar developers. One solar company in particular, PosiGen, is key to the success of the Green Bank's low- to moderate-income incentive programs. Since launching both programs, "solar adoption in low-to-moderate income communities increased by 187%."[28] According to the bank's 2019 legislative report, the bank invested in PosiGen's Connecticut solar lease fund and offered a higher RSIP incentive for those projects that would serve low- and moderate-income customers.[29] The report further notes that low- and moderate-income projects participating in the bank's low- and moderate-income incentive program are 4.4 percent of the overall RSIP program, but that overall participation in the solar program is increasing among low- and moderate-income communities.[30]

These numbers show a remarkable positive trend, but mask the underlying wealth creation occurring for third-party solar companies. The state has created a pathway for broader solar adoption, including in underserved markets like the low- to moderate-income bracket, but third-party companies have dominated the development landscape, which means that the largest economic gains ultimately flow to them. Although implementing solar can allow for a decrease in solar bills of about $450 per year on average for PosiGen's customers,[31] these benefits do not go far enough. Only true ownership and the ability to reap economic benefits at the scale of the investment tax credit would offer a true reversal of a household's fortunes. Further, the bank's most popular products tend to rely on FICO as a measure of creditworthiness, which creates barriers to broader participation in the homes that need access to clean energy the most. In short, the Green Bank's efforts merit recognition, but the bank's programs fall far short of the ideal.

The Connecticut Green Bank's initiatives extend to home improvements as well. The Commercial Property Assessed Clean Energy program is a financing program that allows building owners to invest in clean energy improvements on their properties and pay back the loan over time through an assessment on their property tax bill.[32] The Green Bank Solar Power Purchase Agreement (PPA) uses a multiyear PPA to finance energy projects for commercial customers including businesses, nonprofit organizations, and government agencies.[33] The Small Business Energy Advantage (SBEA) program offers an on-bill commercial energy efficiency program for small businesses. In the SBEA program, the Green Bank provides credit support to help the small businesses attract low-cost financing from Amalgamated Bank, a partner in the program.[34] Another loan program, Smart-E Loan, is a residential loan program that provides access to affordable capital for homeowners to finance property improvements and energy projects.[35] The bank also offers financing for certain multifamily property projects as well as technologically innovative projects.[36] So far, the Green Bank has not released data concerning the impact of these loan programs in low- to moderate-income communities, but they demonstrate positive strides.

New York Green Bank

In 2013, two years after the establishment of the Connecticut Green Bank, across the border in New York, the New York Public Service Commission (NY PSC) approved the establishment of the New York Green Bank, a $1 billion state-sponsored investment fund that is a division of the New York State Energy Research and Development Authority.[37]

The Green Bank's mission is to help "clean energy technologies gain economies of scale" and attract private capital investment.[38] The initial financing of the bank came through an assortment of ratepayer-funded programs, including energy efficiency and renewable energy. In its order establishing the bank, the PSC refused to prescribe a target audience for the deployment of the bank's funds, and left it to the bank to determine how to meet the needs of the state's sizable low- to moderate-income population through its initiatives.[39] To date, the bank has engaged in a range of financing activities, including rooftop solar and energy efficiency, but it has not focused on increasing solar access for utility ratepayers in marginalized communities.

Hawaiʻi GEMS Program

The same year New York established its green bank, the Hawaiʻi legislature enacted Green Energy Market Securitization (GEMS) legislation to establish a green infrastructure financing program to facilitate the state's transition to 100 percent clean energy by 2045.[40] The state's Department of Energy created the GEMS program to respond to the needs of low- to moderate-income clean energy access issues. In 2013, the program's key goals were to:

1. Address financing market barriers to increase the installation of clean energy projects and infrastructure to meet the State's clean energy goals. . . .
2. Democratize clean energy by expanding access and affordability of renewable energy and energy efficiency projects for identified underserved markets, while expanding the market generally;
3. Enable more ratepayers to reduce their energy use and energy costs by helping them finance clean energy improvements;
4. Partner with and support existing market entities in the clean energy and financing sector to ensure GEMS can bridge market

gaps and facilitate a sustainable and efficient private sector market; and

5. Balance the aforementioned goals and objectives with repayment risk to achieve an appropriate rate of return and build a sustainable financing program.[41]

In 2013, utility ratepayers financed the GEMS program through a $150 million bond to be repaid on all utility customer bills over time. The program held great promise as a vehicle to bring access to clean energy to a larger portion of the state's population. Unfortunately, the program never fully got off the ground. Initially, the program struggled to determine its identity. Would it focus on the low- to moderate-income market or simply target condo and apartment dwellers? What would be the repayment interest rate provided for borrowers under the program? Finally, how would individuals or businesses qualify for participation in the program?

I was fortunate enough to be in Hawai'i during the early days of the GEM program. Like many others, I hoped that a program financed by ratepayers would indeed allow for more democratic access to clean energy in the communities that needed it the most. I was wrong. The program floundered and leaned into the moderate- to high-income market as opposed to low-income communities and communities disproportionately burdened by high energy costs. For example, most early GEMS customers fell into income brackets above $100,000 and lived in areas with incomes above 80 percent of the area median income.[42]

Scandal also plagued the program.[43] Despite failing to make any significant loans within three years of being established, the principal amount within the GEMS fund continued to diminish.[44] Administrative fees associated with maintaining the infrastructure of the program ate into the overall amount available for loans, and the program fixated on credit scores as a gateway for participation in the program. Eventually, the state Public Utilities Commission dissolved and reestablished GEMS under the state's energy office.[45] Since September 2019, the program has pivoted back to serving low- and moderate-income ratepayers and has allocated 20 percent of program funds for that purpose.[46] Small businesses, multifamily rental projects, and nonprofit organizations receive the remaining allocation of program funds, and bill payment history, rather than credit score, serves as one of the program qualifications. It is too early to tell whether the programmatic changes made significant impacts on Hawai'i's low- to moderate-income ratepayers, but changes in the program structure indicate a willingness to reach those most in need of the economic and environmental benefits of clean energy.

Green banks initially held incredible promise as the pathway for broader access to clean energy financing for low- to moderate-income energy customers. Although Connecticut's successful program has increased the penetration of solar in low- to moderate-income communities and communities of color, the economic benefits have primarily flowed to corporate entities. New York's program does not focus in any significant way on providing widespread access to finance for the state's low-income communities and communities of color, despite the state's tremendous need. By most early accounts, Hawai'i's program was an outright failure and waste of public funds, but the program may have corrected its course to provide for more distribution of its ratepayer funds.

Pathways to Free Up Income Streams for Marginalized Ratepayers

Like my mother, most low-income families prioritize the essentials: shelter, food, and electricity.[47] Legislators and policy makers should design legislation, financial instruments, and policy guidelines with this fundamental truth in mind. Practically, this means reducing energy burden and ensuring that financial instruments are designed to reach the most economically distressed ratepayers. The cost of solar is rapidly decreasing alongside reduced tax incentives for investment in clean energy. Although reduced tax incentives might lower interest in solar investments, the change in law could create opportunities for creative policy design. The following strategies and policy recommendations offer pathways to free up income streams for low- to moderate-income families, as well as ways for both policy makers and financial institutions to broaden access to finance in the most underserved populations.

Place a Cap on the Percentage of Overall Income that Low- to Moderate-Income Households Pay

Many low- to moderate-income people are currently so burdened by energy costs that they cannot begin to imagine participating in the clean energy transition. Before such families and individuals can avail themselves of the technological innovations of clean energy, the energy system itself must offer economic breathing room in a more equitable way. Policy makers can consider energy prices, or tariffs, that actually take into account the income level of ratepayers. For example, tariffs could set a percentage cap on energy expenditures based on a household's overall income. The cap would operate as a ceiling for energy costs for low- to moderate-income households, meaning that the maximum amount they would pay for electricity would be based on income and not exceed a certain percentage of overall household income. This ceiling could be 6 percent, which is the amount beyond which energy costs become a significant burden for families. The cap could also be reduced to 3 or 4 percent to account for the environmental burdens historically borne by frontline communities.

The policy could also set a flat minimum payment rate for higher-income customers, who tend to pay a lower percentage of their overall income to meet household energy needs. For wealthier customers, the

6 percent would operate as a floor. High-income households would pay, at a minimum, 6 percent of household income for their electricity. For any energy use beyond a certain predetermined usage threshold, the higher-income household would pay an additional fee. In this way, the cost of energy would be distributed more equitably among those who can afford to pay and those who cannot. Although this formulation is somewhat radical, it is the true meaning of equity. In fact, some utility reform advocates have already quietly begun to advocate for such policy design.[48]

Setting a cap on expenditures for low- to moderate-income customers and a floor on expenditures for higher-income customers reflects principles of economic justice. Such a policy would free up 15 to 25 percent of real income for the lowest-income, most impoverished utility customers, who typically also bear the most substantial environmental burdens of the energy system. It might also create excess funds that could be used by low- to moderate-income ratepayers to invest in distributed energy in their communities.

Compensate Communities for Environmental Burdens

Advocates should also press for quantification of environmental burdens on electricity bills. The US Environmental Protection Agency, as well as some states, like California, Massachusetts, and Pennsylvania, have developed mapping tools that allow policy makers to identify the most environmentally burdened communities in a region, state, or locality. Policy makers focused on energy issues should begin to consider energy costs and utility rates with such burdens in mind. Communities affected by energy development (including clean energy development) should receive compensation through their monthly energy bill to account for the environmental, health, and social burdens associated with the energy system. Legislators could legislate this requirement, and policy makers could direct utilities to include a reduction on energy bills based on the burdens a particular community faces. Calculations could be determined by census tract or even more granularly, by community. Utilities would work directly with regulators and third parties to determine the actual costs of the burden and subtract these costs from the overall kilowatt-hour rate charged to customers within the identified area.

This novel formulation would operate as one measure of economic justice for burdened communities and also as recognition justice. The economic justice embedded in this proposal would free up income and reduce energy burden. The recognition justice would acknowledge the unique, sustained, and devastating impacts of the energy system on Black, Brown, and Indigenous communities. The legal framework would also be designed to provide for the escalation of the compensation rate over time, forcing the polluting industry to internalize the cost of its harm, which would also provide a measure of justice: environmental justice.

Create New Formulations for "Creditworthiness"

Even state-funded programs designed to increase access to financing for energy projects fall prey to the constraints of the credit score, and in at least one green bank case, GEMS, this overreliance has limited the bank's success. Race is deeply embedded within the broader discourse surrounding creditworthiness. Redlining refers to the government-sanctioned segregation based on race and access to credit. As Richard Rothstein eloquently details in *The Color of Law*, the US government created the Federal Housing Administration (FHA) in 1934 to increase housing stock around the country.[49] The FHA refused to insure mortgages in Black communities and relied on elaborate maps that designated, in red, which communities were high risk. Black communities, even if middle class, were designated in red and therefore excluded from the federal insurance program. The FHA intentionally focused on increasing access to homeownership in White communities, including going so far as to provide subsidies to home builders in certain communities as long as the homes were not sold to Black persons.[50] These explicitly racist policies excluded generations of Black people from accessing an essential key to wealth creation, homeownership. As with the American dream of homeownership, a dream of community ownership and control of clean energy resources is well within our reach and provides a pathway to wealth creation, but unlocking access to vital resources to build community wealth remains elusive. We need explicitly antiracist financial instruments that aim to undo the troubling legacy of policies like redlining and the discourse of creditworthiness that succeeded it.

Although creditworthiness supposedly measures an individual's likelihood of repaying a loan, the existing metrics used to determine it fail to account for the priorities of low- to moderate-income families. Shelter, food, and energy are basic needs that families prioritize above other expenses.[51] We need new approaches to measure so-called creditworthiness that highlight these priorities. Solstice Solar, a solar company and separate non-profit organization based in Cambridge, Massachusetts, has seized on this gap. The company has endeavored to create a "better, more inclusive qualification standard" beyond the FICO credit score typically used by solar developers to determine creditworthiness.[52]

Solstice has created a metric specifically geared toward participation in community solar projects, the EnergyScore, which is designed to "predict future payment behavior more accurately than FICO credit scores, while simultaneously including a larger proportion of qualified low-to-moderate income customers."[53] In 2020, the EnergyScore was under development, and the company was actively seeking customers to test the metric. The EnergyScore reflects one intervention and innovation that could possibly move the needle for low- to moderate-income communities and broaden access to the financial instruments required for participation in rooftop or community solar programs. PosiGen, the solar company credited with the success of Connecticut's low- to moderate-income solar program, also screens its solar customers based on "home ownership and utility usage history," rather than FICO scores or income, "enabling a population that traditionally has been ignored by the solar sector, and underserved or poorly served by most energy efficiency programs, to access the benefits of clean energy."[54]

Milwaukee, the diverse, struggling city in the heart of the Rust Belt,[55] has also worked to make energy efficiency home improvement programs available to homeowners without relying on credit scores. The Me2 Milwaukee Energy Efficiency program finances energy efficiency–related improvements for homeowners if the property is located in the city limits; the property is a single-family home, duplex, or triplex; the owner is an individual, rather than a business or trust; the property has no delinquent taxes; and the upgrade is done by a participating contractor.[56] Qualified participants must have a one- to two-year record of employment and have a debt-to-income ratio less than 45 percent.[57] The program has no minimum credit score requirement, but those with lower credit scores must have a longer employment history and lower outstanding debts.[58] Although at first blush the program appears less than perfect, using alternative metrics to measure an applicant's ability to pay is a huge step in advancing the equity dimensions of the state's energy efficiency program.

Facilitate On-Bill Financing for Distributed Energy Resources

On-bill financing provides another way for low- to moderate-income utility customers to participate in the energy transition. With on-bill financing, the utility company essentially acts as a bank, amortizing the cost of solar panels (or a community energy project) through the customer's energy bill. Under this scenario, the customer and utility arrange for the customer to pay down the cost of the panels over a period of time, but the monthly cost for the purchasing the panels does not exceed the customer's average utility costs for the year. A third party, such as a solar company, could provide the panels, but receive its payment through the utility bill. In this scenario, the utility would provide a guarantee, or backstop, for the customer's repayment of the underlying solar loan. Alternatively, the utility itself could provide the loan for the panels. In either case, over time, the customer pays down the utility or solar company loan and eventually obtains the ability to generate its electricity under a net metering arrangement.

Such on-bill financing programs already exist. For example, Hawai'i's rebooted GEMS program now provides on-bill financing for "solar and energy efficiency upgrades to renters, low-to-moderate income homeowners, and nonprofits."[59] Under the program, customers repay the investments over time through their electric bill. It is still too early to determine this program's success, but the structure holds promise.

Create Reinvestment and Co-ownership Zones

As the federal investment tax credits begin to sunset and states continue to innovate to meet ambitious clean energy targets, those who make the laws and policies must begin to consider ways to both incentivize clean energy development and equitably distribute the benefits of the development. Lawmakers designed tax credits to incentivize those with large liabilities to participate in clean energy development. These programs attract corporate entities and private parties with sufficient tax appetite. Lawmakers should design the next generation of clean energy tax incentives to require a minimum of community ownership and low- to moderate-income participation in investments. This process may sound unduly complex and burdensome, but it is altogether possible. The South African laws concerning that country's energy transition illustrate this approach.

South Africa emerged from decades of state-sanctioned violence against Black and Brown people determined to ensure the economic inclusion of the most marginalized populations in the new government as well as economic inclusion in the country's fast-paced transition away from fossil fuels. Clean energy projects that succeed in the country's clean energy auctions must include a minimum of 40 percent South African entity participation and a minimum of 12 percent Black ownership of the company responsible for the development, with a target of 20 percent Black ownership percentage.[60] Communities must own at least 2.5 percent of all projects and often participate at higher rates.[61] This policy design, although imperfect, not only offers an entry point for long-struggling communities to benefit from energy projects implemented within their communities, but also acknowledges the necessity for redistribution of wealth to historically marginalized communities. Tax incentives, at either the federal or state level, could be conditioned on similar participatory metrics. Companies should not be able to avail themselves of tax benefits without actively distributing economic benefits to local or affected communities.

Changing the lived energy experiences of marginalized communities will not only require the rapid, widespread deployment of distributed clean energy resources, but it will also require access to the financial instruments that help to lower customer bills and create wealth. For too long, such financial instruments have been the province of the elite. Financiers and even energy policy makers have blithely excluded large swaths of the population from participating in the energy transition by relying on measures of creditworthiness, like FICO, that are themselves infected with racial bias. Revolutionary power requires the exposure of all the ways the economics baked into energy law and policy—through investment tax credits, high electricity rates, and customer-financed green banks—structurally exclude marginalized customers. Only then can households like the one I grew up in stop shuffling bills and start on the pathway to economic freedom.

Conclusion:
Revolutionary Power

Hawai'i—2035

In the end, the waters changed Hawai'i. A storm larger and more devastating than Katrina, Sandy, Harvey, or Maria reshaped the people's sense of place. Hurricane Xavier betrayed Hawai'i's fragile security. Xavier started its journey in late July, wending through the Pacific Ocean away from the South American continent.

For years, hurricanes had danced in the distant South Pacific, eventually making landfall in the Hawaiian Islands as weakened tropical storms or skirting the islands altogether. These early storms caused heavy rains and momentary sewage outfalls into ocean waters, and then they quickly faded into memory. The tourists always returned. Surfers reclaimed local haunts. The ships, laden with oil, food, and a handful of days of the islands' essentials, kept coming.

But 2035 was different. In the days leading up to Xavier, the islands' residents performed a familiar ritual. They flocked to Costco stores, filled their cupboards with nonperishable goods—canned this or that, popcorn, junk food, and, of course, toilet paper and bottled water.

Following Hurricane Katrina in 2005, the US Department of Homeland Security guidance suggested that each resident stock seven days of food and water in their home. For the affluent, this prescription went more unheeded than not. For the poor and low income, such preparation was impossible. Hawai'i is one the most isolated places on Earth; few believed that the islands would be seriously impacted by Xavier, and so residents only prepared half-heartedly.

On July 27, when it became clear that the islands would inevitably sustain a direct hit, the ships stopped coming. Perhaps more devastating than the despoiled beaches, snarled highways, and sewage concerns was the pervasive sense of panic at the prospect of a prolonged shortage of food, medical supplies, and water. Electric company executives also feared that the aging, centralized electricity grid would not survive the storm, so they distributed gas-powered generators to community centers and schools, hoping it would be enough for folks to weather the storm's aftermath. The ultrawealthy boarded private jets to make the dangerous journey toward land. Medically vulnerable residents evacuated their homes for community centers reliant on gas generators. Most families across the islands simply hunkered down, hoping for the best.

In 2019, the administrator for the State of Hawai'i Emergency Management Agency requested the Pacific Disaster Center to complete Category 4 hurricane modeling for Oahu. In public remarks, the administrator said, "The damage would be $116 billion, 159,000 Oahu people (23,000 older than 64) would need short-term shelter, and over 8 million tons of debris on roads would have to be cleared. Hawai'i has a three-day supply of medicine and a five-day supply of real food."[1] The result of a sustained hit by a Category 4 hurricane would devastate the island's economy, infrastructure, and people. Xavier's harm outstripped experts' most nightmarish predictions.

On July 30, 2035, Xavier made landfall. The hurricane was massive. At its peak, it stretched nearly three hundred miles across. Like Katrina, the hurricane hovered and fueled itself with the ocean's warming waters. With wind speeds of more than 150 miles per hour, the storm made landfall with a sustained force that devastated most structures throughout the islands. It dumped more rain than Harvey, a record 100 inches over five days. At the storm's peak, roads merged with waterways that consumed businesses and homes in low-lying areas.

The storm left an indelible mark on the nation's fiftieth state, an archipelago of islands shaped by volcanoes arrayed against the South Pacific in a half-moon shape. The storm exposed the vulnerabilities that many had warned of for decades. The vulnerable suffered immensely. The water-food-energy nexus came into sharp relief. For a short time, a disorienting chaos took hold.

Oahu, the state's most populated island, containing more than 65 percent of the state's 1.4 million residents, felt the losses most profoundly. When the hurricane hit, the island only had around two weeks' worth of food supplies on hand, much of that fresh food that quickly spoiled in the summer heat. In the Waianae community along the island's western coast, the sustained high winds and the heavy rainfall rendered the oil-fired power plant that had defined the community for decades inoperable. The plant, located seven miles from the trash-burning power plant in the same community, burned oil to create more than half of the island's electricity. In the extensive flooding, the facility caught fire and exploded, cutting power to Waikiki, downtown Honolulu, and communities supported by the plant. The storm ripped out the island's centralized grid, held together by a system of aging poles and wires. The wind turbines erected on the island's north shore were not built to withstand the winds of Xavier. They, too, fell into disrepair.

In a virtual blackout, residents found themselves wading through waist-deep streams in search of food, clean water, and high ground. Many died on this search. Many died in their homes, waiting for provisions, electricity, and food to arrive. With limited and expensive gas supplies, the community centers and schools shuttered their doors to local residents.

The power outage also forced the largest uncontrolled flow of sewage into the ocean in the state's history. The sewage, from Oahu's secondary wastewater treatment facility, also located in the low-income community of Waianae, flowed uncontrolled for several weeks, making the popular beaches along the entire south side of Oahu unsafe and undesirable.

Water consumed and devastated. The tides pulled water into sewage drain pipes up through sinks and bathtubs, creating safety hazards in the dense developments and tourist areas along the coast. The storm forced the evacuation of wealthy residents in Honolulu's ill-conceived Kaka'ako development, a luxury urban development project sandwiched between Waikiki to the east and downtown Honolulu to the west. Xavier's endless waters also flooded the principle runways of the islands' main entry point, Honolulu International Airport, long known for its vulnerabilities. For several months, flights could not enter or leave the islands, leaving thousands stranded on either side of the Pacific.

Oahu's main vehicular arteries, H-1 (which connected west and east) and the Pali Highway (connecting north and south) suffered from flooding and landslides, respectively, complicating the island's traffic patterns and the economic flows that rely on them. Service industry workers and medical personnel living west and in the center of Oahu simply could not travel to work, leaving hotels, hospitals, retail businesses, and essential services unstaffed. The train remained functional, but a fundamentally flawed transit design meant that the train did little to connect population centers to the commercial heart of the island.

Moloka'i, a short distance from Oahu, fared a bit better than its wealthier neighbor. After Xavier leveled most of the island's infrastructure and knocked out power, the owner of a Moloka'i solar and battery project filed for bankruptcy and essentially abandoned its assets. With ingenuity and working together, Moloka'i residents repaired the large solar project over a period of several weeks and reconnected it to the grid. The island's small size contributed to the quicker recovery, although some parts of the grid never fully recovered. The community's tight bonds and reliance on subsistence farming and fishing also averted the loss of life experienced on Oahu in the months after the storm.

Even after Hawai'i's recovery, government officials could not avoid the media spotlight on the state's water quality and ongoing infrastructure problems. Tourism, the state's economic engine, slowed to a trickle and then a drip. For would-be tourists, the recent spike in the cost of oil after 2035 made flying a carefully considered investment, and many found the prospect of flying to an island paradise only to avoid swimming at the beach and face rolling blackouts and uncertainty concerning food and water supplies disconcerting.

So, Hawai'i slowly remade itself. Nonenergy experts soon realized that the state's fragile energy system and the system of law and regulation that created it exacerbated the state's collective vulnerability to Hurricane Xavier. These stakeholders also realized that heavy reliance on the state's primary utility to drive energy planning and innovation had led to an unequal system, a system that placed little emphasis on ensuring that marginalized communities had access to clean, reliable, and resilient energy sources. As a result, people in these communities died in disproportionate numbers during and after Hurricane Xavier.

After the hurricane, the state faced difficult policy choices, trade-offs, and financial losses. The state legislature directed the public utilities commission to reopen regulatory proceedings relating to rooftop solar, community energy, and access to financing in low- to moderate-income communities like those along the Waianae coast on Oahu's west side. But in a weakened post-Xavier landscape, it was too late for Hawai'i to orchestrate significant structural change. Struggle and resource shortages defined the process to remake the state's entire electricity system. In the face of the extraordinary damage caused by Hurricane Xavier, the much maligned and beleaguered investor-owned Hawaiian Electric Company, or HECO, folded, selling its assets to a mix of electric cooperatives scattered throughout the state and the City of Honolulu.

It took nearly two decades for Hawai'i to create a new energy system. The people of Hawai'i excavated the ancient lessons from Hawai'i's forefathers and foremothers to build an energy system grounded in broad participation and community-led management of local resources. Hurricane Xavier forced a deep reckoning with the state's inequality and how the energy system had contributed to that inequality. It revealed the connections among the state's energy system and the social and economic power it distributed. The hurricane accelerated regulatory and technological innovation, but it also ensured that equity was central to that innovation.

What Went Wrong?

After Xavier, many of Hawai'i's energy veterans—former utility executives, environmental advocates, solar industry insiders—looked back on the many failed opportunities to create a more just energy system. In the net energy metering fights of the 2010s, regulators agreed to modify the state's rooftop solar program and make it less attractive for low- to moderate-income utility customers to participate in the program. They followed the playbook designed by ALEC in concert with investor-owned utilities. The decision to limit access to rooftop solar programs affected communities in the greatest need of economic support to defray energy costs as well as backup power in the event of power outages.

Observers of Xavier's damage also recalled the complexity and failures associated with the state's community-based renewable energy program, a program that never fully got off the ground and never served as a mechanism for communities to own and manage their own energy. Households that did participate in the community-based renewable energy program more often than not bought a share in a large energy project located far away from their home. When Xavier struck, large solar projects allocated to community-based renewable energy program participants fell prey to the vulnerability of the broader electricity grid. They were located far from customers who could not connect to the disrupted grid. Energy stakeholders lamented the failure of regulators to ensure that the community-based renewable energy program contained strict requirements for locally sited, small-scale energy projects that included incentives for energy storage.

The families in the state juggling electricity bills and the high cost of food and shelter eventually joined the ranks of those in the energy conversation. They, and their advocates, saw their communities suffer in higher numbers in the wake of the hurricane than wealthier communities. They fought against the injustice inherent in the utility compact, which guarantees shareholder returns and allows utilities to raise rates even among low-income customers. When HECO filed for bankruptcy, they organized to create their own version of a justice-oriented electric utility. At that point, the utility's assets were worth so little that they obtained grid infrastructure at a steal. The utility executives and managers who remained in the state scattered throughout the islands and, as a type of penance, offered technical assistance to communities trying to get their community-owned utilities off the ground. Many former executives openly agreed that the system should have been broken up decades ago to allow for greater innovation and different ownership models around the state. That might have allowed certain communities to prioritize important community assets, such as hospitals and community centers, over others when creating a backup power system for emergencies. This diversified and decentralized ownership structure might have also prevented the loss of life.

No one wants this version of our future, but in countless places around the United States—New Orleans, New York, Florida, Nebraska, California, Houston, Puerto Rico, and so many more—a version of this narrative has already played out. In these places, storms and storm surges, floods, fires, and unprecedented weather events have left deep scars on the physical landscape and the collective psyche of impacted communities. These events have left communities without power. They have brought people out into the streets in search of food and water. They have illustrated the exquisite links among climate, poverty, and the structure of the energy system. But these events were not significant enough to spur a transformation of the energy system.

Energy policy is not a panacea, but it is a critical battleground with the potential to mitigate the harms that will come with an unpredictable climate. It is a forum for redistributing wealth and power. Hawai'i eventually learned these lessons, but not without great costs.

Fortunately, it is not too late to create a different future.

The United States—2020–2035

In early 2020, a new coronavirus—SARS-CoV-2, or COVID-19—flayed open the United States, laying bare the vast inequalities that exist at every level of society. The coronavirus pandemic began slowly and crested into wave after wave in the 2020s throughout the nation. With a singular focus, the virus targeted poor and working-class people, Native American communities, and immigrant and Black communities. They were the ones who stocked shelves, cared for the sick, drove buses, operated subways, packed meat, picked vegetables, and cleaned all the places where this work was done. They lived in crowded, multigenerational housing, waiting for the next paycheck to avert eviction or avoid an electricity shutoff; they couldn't afford to be sick. Both documented and undocumented immigrants found themselves in harm's way, disproportionately represented in many of the most dangerous, yet essential, jobs or crowded into detention facilities that lacked even the most basic of amenities like running water and soap. The virus festered in the prisons, filled with Black and Brown bodies that traveled through the state-sanctioned cradle-to-prison pipeline. The virus targeted the country's smugness, too. It shattered the illusion of American dreams, mobility, equality, and exceptionalism. Structural racism, and the policies that undergird it, facilitated much of the havoc wrought by the virus.

Early on, the Centers for Disease Control and Prevention said that people "with serious underlying medical conditions—like serious heart conditions, chronic lung disease, and diabetes, for example—also seem to be at higher risk of developing severe" virus-related illness.[2] Those of us who live and work in environmental justice communities and who study the devastating health and social impacts of the fossil fuel system on communities of color immediately knew what studies would soon reveal: the virus was coming for us.

As it turns out, the majority of the preexisting conditions that increased the risk of death for COVID-19 were the same diseases that were "affected by long-term exposure to air pollution."[3] An early study found that even a small increase in exposure to fine particulate matter led to "a large increase in COVID-19 death" rate, results that "underscore the importance of continuing to enforce existing air pollution regulations to protect human health both during and after the COVID-19 crisis."[4] The design of the fossil-fuel based energy system placed Black and Brown bodies at a unique risk to the deadliest impacts of the coronavirus disease.[5]

The virus forced a reckoning with our unequal livelihoods and unjust mortalities. It changed us. The 2020s was our last decade to take dramatic action on climate change,[6] and in that decade, we finally began to act. We heeded the warning shot fired by a tiny virus. The virus served as a preview for the death, unrest, and chaos promised by climate change, and we mobilized ourselves in service of a different type of society. We knew that a transformed energy system needed to form a key component of the new society. So, as we picked up the pieces from the virus, we began to construct an energy system that no longer burdened our communities and shortened our lives.

We got to work. First, we advocated for federal and state laws to expand the economic benefits associated with clean energy investments. Rather than replicating the tax incentives adopted before COVID-19, we convinced lawmakers to create programs that specifically incentivized investments in low- to moderate-income communities and communities that were historically adversely impacted by the fossil fuel system. Lawmakers drafted legislation that not only required investment in marginalized communities, but also required community ownership in investments. Such legislation helped redistribute wealth to impacted communities and build an economic safety net for the most vulnerable members of society.

After the virus, Big Green organizations began to understand that climate change will expose, and then exacerbate, the unequal structure of our society, which will inevitably lead to deeper social strife and widespread unrest. They began to understand that, from both a moral and practical perspective, any legal or regulatory action to mitigate or adapt to climate change must place equity at the center. At the state level, community advocates and Big Greens finally began to forge authentic partnerships that leveraged the expertise of community members alongside the extraordinary legal and financial resources of Big Greens. Important climate and energy legislation and regulatory proceedings used equity as a starting point, rather than as an item to be addressed at the close of the legislative or regulatory proceeding to placate community advocates.

We began to dream into existence an energy system that reduced the impacts of fossil fuels in communities of color. The new system contained a mix of customer-sited energy, community-scale power, and a smattering of large facilities. Careful work in legislative and regulatory proceedings, as well as tireless advocacy, was required to translate our hopes and dreams into technical policy to guide the transformation of the energy system.

The decade of the virus battered utilities. The deep recession caused by virus-related job losses meant that many utility customers could no longer afford to pay for electricity. With hard-fought restrictions on utilities' ability to recover losses on the backs of ratepayers, many utilities filed for bankruptcy and folded, leaving openings for communities and municipalities to convert utility assets into public goods. The public ownership of energy infrastructure meant that community health and cost reduction were prioritized over utility and shareholder profits.

This new framing of the utility business model allowed for innovations in electricity generation. Customers came together to create community-scale, community-sited energy projects that powered their communities. The state financed these projects through individual energy bills, allowing participants to pay down the cost of the energy project over time, much like a home mortgage. Customers owned and operated these projects and eventually received the energy for free, only paying occasional maintenance fees.

Revolutionary Power: The Only Way Forward

By the time the novel coronavirus struck, the amount of carbon dioxide already in the atmosphere had started global temperatures on an upward trajectory that peaked at 2.5 degrees Celsius. The storms—and the fires and the floods—kept coming. But each time we were knocked down, we bounced back into a system, a society, that was more equal, more just. We created a society in which we not only survived, but we all thrived.

Local energy saved us. We designed our laws with robust participation by the communities shaped and scarred by the fossil fuel–based system. We organized ourselves and formed coalitions to make sure that our new system included a focus on job creation and workforce development.

We dismantled the centralized power system. We fought for access to solar power in our communities, owned by us and designed to meet our community needs. We elected officials who understood the energy burdens borne by Indigenous communities, Brown and Black communities, and poor White communities. They legislated to bring much-needed investments in local, clean power to our communities and made sure that we reaped the economic benefits from it. They drafted and passed legislation to amplify our voices.

We outlived investor-owned utilities and in their place erected a range of publicly owned and community-owned energy entities. They ran on our ideas, rather than the desires of shareholders. We built capacity for energy democracy in our communities by educating community members about energy sources, the economics of power, and the system design. The regulators our leaders appointed quietly deconstructed the architecture of investor-owned utilities and diminished their monopoly power over us.

We learned to navigate the policy spaces that were once deemed too technical to warrant community input. We translated our hopes and dreams, and our ancestors' hopes and dreams, into frameworks and institutions that changed our lives for good.

So, when the storms and fires came, we were prepared. The energy system we spent a decade transforming made us freer, more equal, and better able to come back from major weather events. The new system made our families and our public institutions stronger. The new system was one that we shaped, policy by policy, in anticipation of and love for future generations.

We started, and won, a revolution. We learned where the power lived in our energy system and how it had shaped our choices, our health, and our lives before the virus. We did not win the revolution overnight, but we won. In one version of the future, we heed the warning shot fired by a tiny virus. In another, we do not. I am betting on the version of the future that creates a revolution.

The Principles and Tools of Revolutionary Power

It is revolutionary today to speak of love. It is even more revolutionary for a lawyer and law professor to do so. But revolutionary power is, at its core, about love. It is about a love that looks forward—toward future generations, children unnamed, and possibilities unfurling—and a love that looks back—to ancestors hoping, believing, and praying that you might come into existence.

Revolutionary power is also about love for today. It is about choosing to change our energy system to reflect principles of energy justice and energy democracy now, rather than waiting for climate change to force us to change. Revolutionary power makes the radical proposition that low-income communities and communities of color should own, control, and derive economic benefit from their own energy resources. It asserts that the legacy of structural racism and oppression can be dismantled through energy policy.

Revolutionary power requires courage. It requires pushing against the narrative that we must save the planet first before saving the most vulnerable residents on it. We can and must do both, even when it is slow and even when it is frustrating. Revolutionary power is centering voices that are at the margins of every important conversation concerning energy. It is dismantling power, piece by piece, and erecting an energy system that works for us all.

This book argues that energy policy should be the domain where we fight for the next generation of civil rights. For too long, the design of the energy system has structurally excluded marginalized communities from the policy-making process; imposed unconscionable health and environmental burdens on Black, Brown, Indigenous, and poor White communities; and saddled the most economically strapped households with the highest energy costs. The system does not require these features, and we have entered a window of time when key aspects of the system are being redesigned. As we've seen, several policy areas—utility reform, greenhouse gas legislation and ambitious energy targets, rooftop solar; community energy, and access to finance—are in a great state of flux, and now is the time to act. The policy areas discussed in this book offer pathways to redistribute the power embedded within the energy system to those who have long been burdened by it.

Utility Reform

The investor-owned utility model does not advance energy democracy. Meaningful utility reform offers the promise of lower electricity bills, cleaner air, and greater overall system reliability. Communities and advocates must fight to ensure that the investor-owned utility model innovates and works for them or fight for and advance different business models of electricity generation and distribution. Today, electric cooperatives, public power providers, distributed system operators, and community choice aggregators offer alternatives to the ubiquitous IOU, but the future utility may look nothing like anything we have ever seen. The most important features to promote for that future utility are community participation in governance, a commitment to eliminating environmental burdens in marginalized communities through investments in community-scale and customer-sited clean energy, and a deep commitment to reducing energy burden.

Ambitious Energy and Climate Targets

If we are to solve the climate problem, we have to solve our inequality problem along with it. For decades, climate and environmental advocates have argued for the reverse. This book has shined a light on the ways that climate and renewable energy policies can replicate inequality by failing to center equity. These policies offer the chance to eradicate inequality in our new energy system, but doing so requires extraordinary vigilance and new alliances. Revolutionary power requires frontline advocates and traditional environmental organizations to partner on platforms that insist on justice as a cornerstone of legislative and policy frameworks. This deep partnership is perhaps our greatest chance to recalibrate the power dimensions of climate and energy advocacy.

Rooftop Solar

We have to fight for distributed energy. Conservative interests backed by the fossil fuel industry are fighting mightily to limit and scale back rooftop solar programs just as the cost of solar has made the technology accessible to communities beyond the affluent and middle class. The instability that climate change promises—even if we drastically reduce emissions *today*—requires a deep commitment to distributed energy resources, including the prioritization of rooftop solar and battery storage in our most vulnerable communities. Going forward, energy policy must privilege frontline communities in accessing rooftop solar and ensure that the programs offer meaningful economic benefits.

Community Energy

Our energy transition has left many behind. Renters, low-income people, and those with inadequate rooftops have not been able to participate in rooftop solar programs. Community energy will not solve all our energy problems, but it will give communities the opportunity to come together to create renewable energy projects that reduce harmful emissions and generate community wealth. Community energy comes in many names, sizes, and flavors, but the devil is in the details. The key to revolutionary power is ensuring community ownership and control, tracking economic benefits, and making sure the project scale and location align with community values.

Access to Finance

Our most economically distressed neighbors pay too much to keep their households afloat, and they have been willfully ignored as others move into the clean energy future. This practice, too, needs to end. Revolutionary power requires a reimagining of the energy burdens borne by marginalized communities. It requires a reshaping of energy rates to reflect historical burdens and offer families a chance to get above water when paying energy bills. Financial institutions creating pathways for local clean energy must simultaneously create pathways for low- to moderate-income participation in clean energy loans. To facilitate this participation, they must move away from traditional measures of credit worthiness, like the credit score, toward innovations such as on-bill financing and bill payment history to make sure that those most burdened by the fossil fuel–based energy system can finally benefit in the clean energy system.

In this book, a series of stories woven throughout with dreams, I have revisited the places that have moved me: Port Arthur, Texas; Oaxaca, Mexico; Hawai'i; and Puerto Rico. I have asked permission of my family to tell their stories and tried to write with authenticity the voices of those whose struggles taught me about energy and power. You, dear reader, are a product of your own stories, the places you have been, and your own ancestors' wildest dreams for your life. Take the tools I have outlined in this book. Arm yourself with them. Make them your own. Use them to create your own revolution. We are rooting for you.

Acknowledgments

Scores of people and communities contributed to the ideas included in this book. Communities in Oaxaca first taught me about a type of justice that does not compromise. A group of students at the University of Hawaiʻi took a gamble on my ideas and helped me launch the Energy Justice Program at the Richardson School of Law. Claire, Sean, Tim, Arielle, and James—together we learned about Hawaiʻi's energy landscape and began to dream up the architecture of energy justice. Our work together formed the foundation of *Revolutionary Power*.

Henry Curtis, Sarah Krakoff, Nathan Phelps, and Shelley Welton read early drafts of this book and provided invaluable feedback. My editor at Island Press, Heather Boyer, also read and commented on countless sketches and drafts. Her prodding gave me the courage to tell the stories found in this book.

I owe particular gratitude to Subin DeVar and Shiva Prakash, my cofounders at the Initiative for Energy Justice. Their intellectual comradery and partnership for the past several years has inspired and encouraged me. This book reflects many of our hopes and dreams and offers a glimpse into how we might fight for them.

I have written this book over the course of many years. The writing process involved remembering anecdotes, reviewing notes scribbled in the margins of regulatory filings and orders, and leaning on many eager and patient research assistants. I relied heavily on Ana Doherty, Andrew Kinde, and Alexis Laundry to fill in many of the gaps in my research. Karl Meakin not only offered impeccable research assistance, but he also ensured that this book made it across the finish line.

My partner stood by (and back) as I struggled to pen this book. I cannot return the many vacations and late nights stolen from us in my pursuit of this dream, but I won't forget her immeasurable sacrifices. I could not have asked for a better cheerleader, listener, and sounding board. This book benefited from her edits, critiques, and love.

I owe my family everything. They gave me my stories—and a voice to tell them.

Notes

Introduction

1. According to the National Oceanic and Atmospheric Administration, National Centers for Environmental Information, the "five warmest years in the 1880–2019 record have all occurred since 2015, while nine of the 10 warmest years have occurred since 2005." NOAA, "Global Climate Report," National Centers for Environmental Information, 2019, https://www.ncdc.noaa.gov/sotc/global/201913.

2. IPCC, "Summary for Policymakers," Global Warming of 1.5°C. An IPCC Special Report on the Impacts of Global Warming of 1.5°C above Pre-Industrial Levels and Related Global Greenhouse Gas Emission Pathways, in the Context of Strengthening the Global Response to the Threat of Climate Change, Sustainable Development, and Efforts to Eradicate Poverty, 2018, https://www.ipcc.ch/sr15/.

3. Energy Justice Network, "Principles of Climate Justice," 2009, https://www.ejnet.org/ej/.

Chapter 1. Energy, Energy Justice, and Civil Rights

1. As my sister and my food choices that summer reflect, Port Arthur is also likely a food desert, a community characterized, in part, by limited options for fresh fruit and vegetables. Then again, our food choices may also be a reflection of a new type of freedom and cash, things that were

in short supply in our hometown. For more on food deserts, see USDA Economic Research Service, "Food Access Research Atlas," October 31, 2019, https://www.ers.usda.gov/data-products/food-access-research-atlas /go-to-the-atlas/.

2. Robert D. Bullard et al., "Toxic Wastes and Race at Twenty: Why Race Still Matters after All of These Years," *Environmental Law* 38, no. 2 (2008): 371–411; see also Black Leadership Forum et al., "Air of Injustice: African Americans and Power Plant Pollution," October 2002, https://www.energyjustice.net/files/coal/Air_of_Injustice.pdf, 6. The report states that 68 percent of African Americans live within 30 miles of a power plant, compared to 56 percent of the white population, which lives within 30 miles of a coal-fired power plant.

3. David Schlosberg and Lisette B. Collins, "From Environmental to Climate Justice: Climate Change and the Discourse of Environmental Justice," *Wiley Interdisciplinary Reviews: Climate Change* 5, no. 3 (2014): 359–74.

4. Commission for Racial Justice, "Toxic Wastes and Race in the United States: A National Report on the Racial and Socio-Economic Characteristics of Communities with Hazardous Waste Sites," 1987, https://www .nrc.gov/docs/ML1310/ML13109A339.pdf., archived at https://perma .cc/ETA8-3X5B, xi.

5. Robert D. Bullard, "Dismantling Environmental Racism in the USA," *Local Environment* 4, no. 1 (1999): 5–6.

6. Bullard, "Dismantling Environmental Racism," 6 (emphasis in original).

7. Bullard, "Dismantling Environmental Racism," 13.

8. Executive Order 12898 of February 11, 1994, Federal Actions to Address Environmental Justice in Minority Populations and Low-Income Populations, *Code of Federal Regulations*, title 3 (1994), https://www.archives .gov/files/federal-register/executive-orders/pdf/12898.pdf.

9. Bullard et al., "Toxic Wastes and Race at Twenty." Bullard's team uses 2000 US census data to demonstrate that "people of color and low-income communities are still the dumping ground for all kinds of toxins" and that "hazardous waste host neighborhoods are composed predominantly of people of color" (372).

10. Statistical Atlas, "Race and Ethnicity in Port Arthur, Texas," September 12, 2018, https://statisticalatlas.com/place/Texas/Port-Arthur/Race-and

-Ethnicity, archived at https://perma.cc/KBK6-R3NC (highlighting a majority of zoning blocks in downtown Port Arthur ranging from 77 to 100 percent African American).

11. Statistical Atlas, "Race and Ethnicity in Port Arthur, Texas," September 12, 2018, https://statisticalatlas.com/place/Texas/Port-Arthur/Race-and -Ethnicity, archived at https://perma.cc/R8PC-5CPJ; Trevor Bach, "'Sentenced to Death': What It's Like Living in a Cancer-Plagued Oil Town," VICE, January 2, 2020, https://www.vice.com/en_us/article/3a8nk3 /sentenced-to-death-what-its-like-living-in-a-cancer-plagued-oil-town.

12. Wen Stephenson, "Welcome to West Port Arthur, Texas, Ground Zero in the Fight for Climate Justice," *The Nation*, June 3, 2014, https://www .thenation.com/article/archive/welcome-west-port-arthur-texas-ground -zero-fight-climate-justice/.

13. Data USA, Data USA: Port Arthur, TX, accessed July 21, 2020, https:// datausa.io/profile/geo/port-arthur-tx/#:~:text=30.7%25%20of%20the% 20population%20for,the%20national%20average%20of%2013.1%25; Index Mundi, Texas Poverty Rate by City, accessed July 21, 2020, https:// www.indexmundi.com/facts/united-states/quick-facts/texas/percent-of -people-of-all-ages-in-poverty/cities#chart.

14. Harry Hurt III, "The Cancer Belt," *Texas Monthly*, May 1, 1981, https:// www.texasmonthly.com/articles/the-cancer-belt/; Daniel Yergin, *The Prize: The Epic Quest for Oil, Money, and Power* (New York: Free Press, 1991), chap. 4.

15. Hurt, "The Cancer Belt."

16. Hurt, "The Cancer Belt."

17. Bach, "'Sentenced to Death.'"

18. Bach, "'Sentenced to Death.'"

19. See, for example, Courtney Cherry, "The Keystone Pipeline: Environmentally Just," *Environmental and Energy Law and Policy Journal* 6 (2011): 125.

20. Bach, "'Sentenced to Death.'"

21. Tracking California, "Heart Attacks and the Environment," accessed May 4, 2020, https://trackingcalifornia.org/heart-attacks/heart-attacks-and -the-environment; Brian Kim Juyong et al., "Cumulative Lifetime Burden of Cardiovascular Disease from Early Exposure to Air Pollution," *Journal of the American Heart Association* 9, no. 6 (March 17, 2020): e014944,

https://doi.org/10.1161/JAHA.119.014944; C. Arden Pope et al., "Cardiovascular Mortality and Long-Term Exposure to Particulate Air Pollution," *Circulation* 109, no. 1 (January 6, 2004): 71–77, https://doi.org/10.1161/01.CIR.0000108927.80044.7F.

22. Stephenson, "Welcome to West Port Arthur, Texas."

23. Ellen Knickmeyer, "'They're Killing Us,' Texas Residents Say of Trump Rollbacks," *Washington Post*, April 19, 2020, https://www.washington post.com/climate-environment/theyre-killing-us-texas-residents-say-of -trump-rollbacks/2020/04/19/2a8cc0a2-8259-11ea-81a3-9690c9881111 _story.html.

24. Stephenson, "Welcome to West Port Arthur, Texas."

25. Stephenson, "Welcome to West Port Arthur, Texas."

26. For an in-depth portrait of the environmental harms experienced by Port Arthur residents, see Zed Nelson, *Shelter in Place: Living in the Shadow of the Petrochemical Industry*, 2009, https://www.films.com/id/18226; Zehl & Associates, "Large Fire Breaks Out at Valero Port Arthur Refinery Recently Reopened Following Hurricane Harvey," September 20, 2017, https://www.zehllaw.com/large-fire-breaks-valero-port-arthur-refinery -port-recently-reopened-following-hurricane-harvey/; Ana Parras, "No One Should Have to Breathe These Chemicals," *New York Times*, December 6, 2019, sec. Opinion, https://www.nytimes.com/2019/12/06/opinion /port-neches-tx-explosion.html.

27. Unfortunately, the company terminated these benefits, and Uncle D is back at work as a contractor in the local refineries.

28. In "Anti-Resilience: A Roadmap for Transformational Justice within the Energy System," *Harvard Civil Rights-Civil Liberties Law Review* 54, no. 1 (2019), I discuss Port Arthur and energy justice in greater detail.

29. Denise Fairchild and Al Weinrub, eds., *Energy Democracy: Advancing Equity in Clean Energy Solutions* (Washington, DC: Island Press, 2017), 8 (noting the connection between the fossil fuel economy and slavery, stating that the "rise of fossil fuel power in the last two hundred years was a key factor in replacing the slave system of production with free labor and in industrializing and commercializing the U.S. economy").

30. Ivan Penn, Peter Eavis, and James Glanz, "California Wildfires: How PG&E Ignored Risks in Favor of Profits," *New York Times*, March 18, 2019, sec. Business, https://www.nytimes.com/interactive/2019/03/18 /business/pge-california-wildfires.html.

31. Penn, Eavis, and Glanz, "California Wildfires."

32. Penn, Eavis, and Glanz, "California Wildfires."

33. Penn, Eavis, and Glanz, "California Wildfires."

34. Nishant Kishore et al., "Mortality in Puerto Rico after Hurricane Maria," *New England Journal of Medicine* 379, no. 2 (May 29, 2018): 162–70.

35. David Sheppard and Scott DiSavino, "Superstorm Sandy Cuts Power to 8.1 Million Homes," *Reuters*, October 30, 2012, https://www.reuters.com/article/us-storm-sandy-powercuts-idUSBRE89T10G20121030.

36. Rod Walton, "Ten Years After: How Entergy New Orleans Survived Hurricane Katrina," POWERGrid International, August 24, 2015, https://www.power-grid.com/2015/08/24/ten-years-after-how-entergy-new-orleans-survived-hurricane-katrina/.

37. Raphael J. Heffron and Darren McCauley, "The Concept of Energy Justice across the Disciplines," *Energy Policy* 105 (June 1, 2017): 658–67, https://doi.org/10.1016/j.enpol.2017.03.018.

38. Nancy Leong, "Racial Capitalism," *Harvard Law Review* 126 (2012): 2151.

39. Shalanda H. Baker, "Mexican Energy Reform, Climate Change, and Energy Justice in Indigenous Communities," *Natural Resources Journal* 56, no. 2 (2016): 369–90; Shalanda H. Baker, "Why the IFC's Free, Prior, and Informed Consent Policy Does Not Matter (Yet) to Indigenous Communities Affected by Development Projects," *Wisconsin International Law Journal* 30 (2012): 668.

40. Mary Finley-Brook and Erica L. Holloman draw a similar conclusion in "Empowering Energy Justice," noting that although solar and wind are on the rise globally, benefits are not equitably distributed. Further, energy "transitions highlighting efficiency and cost-effectiveness can reinforce existing social imbalances: In the green energy sector, wealthier populations are more likely to gain, sometimes at the expense of the poor." *International Journal of Environmental Research and Public Health* 13, no. 9 (2016): 926.

Chapter 2. Utility Reform: The Linchpin to Transforming the Energy System

1. Hawaiian Electric, "The Birth of Hawaiian Electric," accessed April 22, 2020, http://www.hawaiianelectric.com/about-us/our-history/1881-the-birth.

As should be evident, I construe the concept of power broadly to encompass political, social, and economic dimensions. Prior to its unlawful annexation to the United States, Hawai'i, as a sovereign entity and collection of individuals, possessed power beyond its ability to light the capitol or eight hundred homes. In the 1830s, literacy rates in the Hawaiian nation exceeded that of the United States. Collectivism reigned, and the land, or 'aina, provided for the people in abundance through a complex resource management system that guaranteed each citizen enough food to eat. By any modern measure, the abundance of natural resources in the Hawaiian nation, home to as many as a million residents, made the nation wealthy and self-sustaining. Indeed, armed with such abundance, Hawai'i's people had power.

2. Average household energy usage in Hawai'i is much lower than the national average, at 518 kilowatt-hours per month, according to the EIA: Energy Information Administration, "2018 Average Monthly Bill–Residential," 2018, https://www.eia.gov/electricity/sales_revenue_price/pdf/table5_a.pdf.

3. US Census Bureau, "The Supplemental Poverty Measure: 2018," October 2019, 28.

4. US Census Bureau, "The Supplemental Poverty Measure: 2018," 28.

5. Public Utilities Commission of the State of Hawai'i, "Decision and Order No. 32052," April 28, 2014.

6. Public Utilities Commission of the State of Hawai'i, "Decision and Order No. 32052," Exhibit A.

7. The precise language the PUC uses is no less direct. The order states, "The Commission is compelled to offer the following perspectives on the vision, business strategies, and regulatory policy changes required to align the HECO Companies' business model with customers' interests and the state's public policy goals. The Commission is compelled because the HECO Companies failed to articulate a sustainable business model in the intervening time period since this directive was set forth by the Commission almost one year ago in Order No. 31288," Exhibit A.

8. Public Utilities Commission of the State of Hawai'i, "Decision and Order No. 32052," Exhibit A, 3.

9. Public Utilities Commission of the State of Hawai'i, "Decision and Order No. 32052," Exhibit A, 1.

10. Nick Brown and Jessica Resnick-Ault, "Puerto Rico Utility Sale Sets Up

Fight with Creditors," *Reuters*, January 24, 2018, https://www.reuters
.com/article/us-puertorico-debt-prepa-analysis-idUSKBN1FD0FP.

11. Cathy Kunkel and Tom Sanzillo, "PREPA Privatization Will Hurt Consumers and Slow Economic Recovery," Institute for Energy Economics
and Financial Analysis, January 2019, https://ieefa.org/ieefa-report-prepa
-privatization-means-crushingly-high-electric-rates/.

12. Ivan Penn and Peter Eavis, "PG&E Reaches Agreement with Governor,
Clearing Bankruptcy Hurdle," *New York Times*, March 20, 2020, sec.
Business, https://www.nytimes.com/2020/03/20/business/energy-environ
ment/pge-deal-gavin-newsom-california.html.

13. Energy Information Administration, "Investor-Owned Utilities Served
72% of U.S. Electricity Customers in 2017," Today in Energy, August 15,
2019, https://www.eia.gov/todayinenergy/detail.php?id=40913.

14. Energy Information Administration, "Electric Sales, Revenue, and Average Price," March 16, 2020, https://www.eia.gov/electricity/sales_revenue
_price/.

15. American Public Power Association, "Public Power for Your Community," 2016, https://www.publicpower.org/system/files/documents
/municipalization-public_power_for_your_community.pdf, 9.

16. American Public Power Association, "Public Power for Your Community," 11.

17. Energy Information Administration, "Electric Power Monthly with Data
for February 2020," April 2020.

18. Energy Information Administration, "Electric Sales, Revenue, and Average Price," March 16, 2020, https://www.eia.gov/electricity/sales_revenue
_price/.

19. American Public Power Association, "Public Power for Your Community," 21.

20. Hannah J. Wiseman and Sara C. Bronin, "Community-Scale Renewable
Energy," *San Diego Journal of Climate and Energy Law* 4 (2013): 176;
James B. Dean and Thomas Earl Geu, "The Uniform Limited Cooperative Association Act: An Introduction," *Drake Journal of Agricultural Law*
13, no. 1 (2008): 66.

21. NRECA, "Understanding the Seven Cooperative Principles," America's
Electric Cooperatives, December 1, 2016, https://www.electric.coop/seven
-cooperative-principles/.

22. Energy Information Administration, "Investor-Owned Utilities Served 72% of U.S. Electricity Customers in 2017," Today in Energy, August 15, 2019, https://www.eia.gov/todayinenergy/detail.php?id=40913.

23. Herman Trabish, "While Some Talk of New Business Models, Iowa's Coops Invent Them," Utility Dive, November 6, 2014, https://www.utilitydive.com/news/while-some-talk-of-new-business-models-iowas-coops-invent-them/329804/.

24. Trabish, "While Some Talk of New Business Models."

25. Trabish, "While Some Talk of New Business Models."

26. NRECA, "America's Electric Cooperatives," April 23, 2019, https://www.electric.coop/wp-content/uploads/2020/05/NRECA-Fact-Sheet-5-2020-1.pdf.

27. Energy Information Administration, "Investor-Owned Utilities Served 72% of U.S. Electricity Customers in 2017."

28. William Boyd, "Public Utility and the Low-Carbon Future," *UCLA Law Review* 61, no. 6 (2014): 1614–711.

29. City of Boulder, "FAQ," Local Power, 2020, https://bouldercolorado.gov/local-power/faq-3.

30. City of Boulder, "FAQ."

31. City of Boulder, "FAQ."

32. American Public Power Association, "Public Power for Your Community."

33. American Public Power Association, "Public Power for Your Community."

34. American Public Power Association, "Public Power for Your Community."

35. American Public Power Association, "Public Power for Your Community," 28–31.

36. State of New York Public Service Commission, "Order Adopting Regulatory Policy Framework and Implementation Plan," February 26, 2015, 31.

37. Davide Savenije, "In New York, Utility of the Future Will Be 'Air Traffic Controller,'" Utility Dive, March 12, 2015, https://www.utilitydive.com/news/in-new-york-utility-of-the-future-will-be-air-traffic-controller/373342/.

38. US EPA, "U.S. Electricity Grid & Markets," Overviews and Factsheets,

August 30, 2017, https://www.epa.gov/greenpower/us-electricity-grid
-markets.

39. John Farrell, "PURPA: A Quiet Death or Longer Life after 40 Years of
Wholesale Electricity Competition?," September 18, 2017, https://www
.greentechmedia.com/articles/read/a-quiet-death-or-longer-life-after-40
-years-of-wholesale-electricity-compet.

40. Karlee Weinmann, "An Overlooked Solution for Competitive and Local
Renewable Power," Institute for Local Self-Reliance, September 6, 2017,
https://ilsr.org/an-overlooked-solution-for-competitive-and-local-renew
able-power/.

41. Energy Information Administration, "Power Marketers Are Increasing
Their Share of U.S. Retail Electricity Sales," Today in Energy, June 12,
2018, https://www.eia.gov/todayinenergy/detail.php?id=36415.

42. Energy Information Administration, "Power Marketers Are Increasing
Their Share."

43. Local Energy Aggregation Network, "CCA by State," accessed May 7,
2020, https://leanenergyus.org/cca-by-state/.

44. Denise Fairchild and Al Weinrub, eds., *Energy Democracy: Advancing
Equity in Clean Energy Solutions* (Washington, DC: Island Press, 2017),
142–43.

45. Fairchild and Weinrub, *Energy Democracy*, 148.

46. Fairchild and Weinrub, *Energy Democracy*, 150.

47. Eric O'Shaughnessy et al., "Community Choice Aggregation: Challenges,
Opportunities, and Impacts on Renewable Energy Markets," NREL,
Luskin Center for Innovation, February 2019, https://www.nrel.gov/docs
/fy19osti/72195.pdf.

48. Robert Walton, "California Decision Means Higher Costs for Community Choice Programs," Utility Dive, October 12, 2018, https://www
.utilitydive.com/news/california-decision-means-higher-costs-for-com
munity-choice-programs/539552/.

Chapter 3. Ending Climate Change Fundamentalism

1. Hawaii Department of Business, Economic Development and Tourism,
"Island Population and Housing Units, State of Hawaii: 2010," June
2011, http://files.hawaii.gov/dbedt/census/Census_2010/PL94-171/
Island_Report_Final.pdf.

2. Molokai Community Health Center, "Population Served," Molokai Health Center, accessed March 25, 2020, http://molokaichc.org/popu lation-served/.

3. US Department of Health and Human Services, Office of the Assistant Secretary for Planning and Evaluation, "2019 Poverty Guidelines," January 11, 2019, https://aspe.hhs.gov/2019-poverty-guidelines.

4. The study, conducted by a number of agencies, including the Hawaiʻi Department of Health, defines food security as "the ready availability of nutritionally adequate and safe foods and the ability to acquire them in socially acceptable ways." Hawaiʻi Department of Health, "Hunger and Food Insecurity in Hawaiʻi: Baseline Estimates," October 2001, 7–8, https://health.hawaii.gov/hhs/files/2013/04/specfood.pdf.

5. Maui Electric, "Average Price of Electricity," accessed March 25, 2020, http://www.mauielectric.com/billing-and-payment/rates-and-regulations /average-price-of-electricity.

6. US Energy Information Administration, "Electric Power Monthly," January 2020.

7. Kathryn Mykleseth, "Wind Power Raises Maui Electric Bills," *National Wind Watch*, April 20, 2017, https://www.wind-watch.org/news/2017/04 /22/wind-power-raises-maui-electric-bills/.

8. Patrick Grady, "Molokai-Lanai Islands Large Land Owners," Data Basin, June 12, 2015, https://databasin.org/maps/a416da68a2b94eb3b0117e03 863d628d/active.

9. Marie D. Strazar, *Molokaʻi in History: A Guide to the Resources* (Honolulu: Hawaiʻi State Foundation on Culture and the Arts, 2000), https://sfca .hawaii.gov/wp-content/uploads/2013/08/Molokai2000_SFCA1.pdf; Erik Weinbrecht, "The Molokai Ranch: Over 55,000 Acres of Historic Hawaiian Paradise," *Sotheby's International Realty* (blog), September 19, 2017, https://www.sothebysrealty.com/extraordinary-living-blog/the -molokai-ranch-over-55000-acres-of-historic-hawaiian-paradise.

10. Weinbrecht, "The Molokai Ranch"; Strazar, *Molokaʻi in History*.

11. Department of Hawaiian Home Lands, "Molokaʻi Island Plan," June 2005, ES-1, https://dhhl.hawaii.gov/wp-content/uploads/2012/05/Island _Plan_Molokai_2005.pdf.

12. Department of Hawaiian Home Lands, "About," accessed March 27, 2020, https://dhhl.hawaii.gov/about/.

13. Kristen Corey et al., "Housing Needs of Native Hawaiians: A Report from the Assessment of American Indian, Alaska Native, and Native Hawaiian Housing Needs" (Washington, DC: US Department of Housing and Urban Development, May 2017), xi, https://www.huduser.gov/portal/sites/default/files/pdf/HNNH.pdf.

14. Department of Hawaiian Home Lands, *Moloka'i Island Plan.*

15. Department of Hawaiian Home Lands, *Moloka'i Island Plan,* 2–6.

16. Statistical Atlas, "Food Stamps in Hawaii," accessed March 27, 2020, https://statisticalatlas.com/state/Hawaii/Food-Stamps.

17. Duane Shimogawa, "Hawaii Undersea Cable Project Still on the Table, HECO Report Says," *Pacific Business News,* February 24, 2016, https://www.bizjournals.com/pacific/news/2016/02/24/hawaii-undersea-cable-project-still-on-the-table.html.

18. Dyani Lewis, "Energy Positive: How Denmark's Samsø Island Switched to Zero Carbon," *The Guardian,* February 23, 2017, sec. Guardian Sustainable Business, https://www.theguardian.com/sustainable-business/2017/feb/24/energy-positive-how-denmarks-sams-island-switched-to-zero-carbon; Diane Cardwell, "Green-Energy Inspiration Off the Coast of Denmark," *New York Times,* January 17, 2015, sec. Business, https://www.nytimes.com/2015/01/18/business/energy-environment/green-energy-inspiration-from-samso-denmark.html.

19. Harmonee Williams, Emillia Noordhoek, and Malia Akutagawa, "Molokai Energy Assessment," Sust'āinable Moloka'i, May 2014, http://www.sustainablemolokai.org/wp-content/uploads/2014/09/SM_Energy-Assessment-with-appendices_May-2014.pdf.

20. Diane Cardwell, "Solar Power Battle Puts Hawaii at Forefront of Worldwide Changes," *New York Times,* April 18, 2015, sec. Business, https://www.nytimes.com/2015/04/19/business/energy-environment/solar-power-battle-puts-hawaii-at-forefront-of-worldwide-changes.html; Herman Trabish, "17% of Hawaiian Electric Customers Now Have Rooftop Solar," Utility Dive, February 1, 2016, https://www.utilitydive.com/news/17-of-hawaiian-electric-customers-now-have-rooftop-solar/413014/.

21. Gopal Dayaneni, "Carbon Fundamentalism vs. Climate Justice," *Race, Poverty and the Environment* 16, no. 2 (Fall 2009): 9.

22. Denise Fairchild and Al Weinrub, eds., *Energy Democracy: Advancing Equity in Clean Energy Solutions* (Washington, DC: Island Press, 2017), 11.

23. Fabian Nunez, "An Act to Add Division 25.5 (Commencing with Section 38500) to the Health and Safety Code, Relating to Air Pollution," Pub. L. No. AB 32 (2006), sec. 38591, http://www.leginfo.ca.gov/pub/05-06/bill/asm/ab_0001-0050/ab_32_bill_20060927_chaptered.pdf.

24. Eileen Gauna, "Environmental Law, Civil Rights and Sustainability: Three Frameworks for Environmental Justice," *Journal of Environmental and Sustainability Law* 19 (2012): 34. (citing comments from the Center on Race, Poverty & Environment that cap and trade "is an ineffective system because it does not require major polluters to reduce their carbon emissions. Cap and Trade allows major emitters of greenhouse gases to buy 'reductions' from other polluters instead of reducing their own emissions by purchasing 'offsets.' Offsets can be bought from a source nearly anywhere in the world and go to fund ecofriendly projects. So while trees are being planted in Canada, corporations can continue to pollute back home in California at levels equal to or even greater than they did before AB 32. Cap and Trade deprives nearby residents from the benefits of toxic, smog, and particulate matter reductions that would accompany local greenhouse gas reductions. Environmental justice communities burdened by huge industrial concentrations of pollution would likely see no benefits when major polluters buy, instead of reduce, their pollution.")

25. Alice Kaswan, "California Climate Policies Serving Climate Justice," American Bar Association, April 23, 2019, https://www.americanbar.org/groups/environment_energy_resources/publications/natural_resources_environment/2018-19/spring/california-climate-policies-serving-climate-justice/.

26. Environmental Justice Advisory Council, "Priority EJAC Recommendations and CARB Responses," May 23, 2017. Food and Water Watch and a few other organizations have also advocated for abandoning the cap-and-trade program in favor of regulatory/nonmarket approaches; see, for example, https://www.foodandwaterwatch.org/sites/default/files/ibsp_1711_ejpaytopollute-webfin2_0.pdf.

27. Nunez, "An Act to add Division 25.5."

28. Nicholas Stump, "Mountain Resistance: Appalachian Civil Disobedience in Critical Legal Research Modeled Law Reform," *Environs: Environmental Law and Policy Journal* 41 (2017): 69 (referring to the Big Greens).

29. Equitable and Just National Climate Platform, "A Vision for an Equitable and Just Climate Future," accessed July 6, 2020, https://ajustclimate.org/.

30. Equitable and Just National Climate Platform, "A Vision."

31. Equitable and Just National Climate Platform, "A Vision."

32. Equitable and Just National Climate Platform, "A Vision."

33. Hawai'i Revised Statutes, Section 269-91 Definitions (2020), https://www.capitol.hawaii.gov/hrscurrent/Vol05_Ch0261-0319/HRS0269/HRS_0269-0091.htm.

34. Public Utilities Commission of the State of Hawai'i, Docket No. 2015-0022—Application of Hawaiian Electric Companies and NextEra Energy for Approval of the Proposed Change of Control and Related Matters, Applicants' Response to LOL-RI-234, June 15, 2015, 2.

35. Public Utilities Commission of the State of Hawai'i, "Decision and Order No. 35609," July 30, 2018, https://dms.puc.hawaii.gov/dms/DocumentViewer?pid=A1001001A18G31B13357J00028.

36. Molokai New Energy Partners, "Benefits the Project Provides to Molokai," accessed April 3, 2020, https://molokai.solar/what-the-project-means.

37. Lee Imada, "Solar-Battery Project OK'd," August 2, 2018, https://www.mauinews.com/news/local-news/2018/08/solar-battery-project-okd/; Kehaulani Cerizo, "Lanai, Molokai Focus of Renewable Energy Projects," August 15, 2019, https://www.mauinews.com/news/local-news/2019/08/lanai-molokai-focus-of-renewable-energy-projects/.

38. Molokai New Energy Partners, "Benefits the Project Provides to Molokai."

39. Molokai New Energy Partners, "About the Team," accessed April 4, 2020, https://molokai.solar/about-the-team.

40. At the time of this writing, the project had not broken ground. Sust'ainable Moloka'i and other parties have initiated litigation to force the developer to fulfill its contract to build the project.

41. Arielle Swernoff, "Statement on the Climate Leadership and Community Protection Act," NY Renews, June 18, 2019.

42. Swernoff, "Statement."

43. Swernoff, "Statement."

44. Swernoff, "Statement."

45. Swernoff, "Statement."

46. Todd Kaminsky, "Climate Leadership and Community Protection Act," S. 6599 (2019), https://www.nysenate.gov/legislation/bills/2019/s6599.

47. Kaminsky, Climate Leadership and Community Protection Act.

48. Kaminsky, Climate Leadership and Community Protection Act.

49. Kaminsky, Climate Leadership and Community Protection Act.

50. Kaminsky, Climate Leadership and Community Protection Act.

51. Kaminsky, Climate Leadership and Community Protection Act.

52. The 100% Network, "Comprehensive Building Blocks for a Regenerative and Just 100% Policy," January 2020. The manual is available for download at https://www.100percentnetwork.org/uploads/cms/documents /100-network_comprehensive-building-blocks-for-a-just-regenerative-100 -policy-2020.pdf.

53. The 100% Network, "Comprehensive Building Blocks."

54. The 100% Network, "Comprehensive Building Blocks."

Chapter 4. The Fight for Local Power

1. Interviewee in discussion with the author's research team, Puerto Rico, April 16, 2019. Audio on file with the author.

2. John Wargo, *Green Intelligence* (New Haven, CT: Yale University Press, 2009), chap. 6, www.jstor.org/stable/j.ctt1nps02.

3. 46 U.S.C. 50101 et seq.; US Energy Information Administration, "Electric Power Monthly," January 2020.

4. Interviewee in discussion with the author's research team, Puerto Rico, October 24, 2018. Audio on file with the author.

5. Nishant Kishore et al., "Mortality in Puerto Rico after Hurricane Maria," *New England Journal of Medicine* 379, no. 2 (May 29, 2018): 162–70; Raul Cruz-Cano and Erin L. Mead, "Causes of Excess Deaths in Puerto Rico After Hurricane Maria: A Time-Series Estimation," *American Journal of Public Health* 109, no. 7 (April 18, 2019): 1050–52, https://doi.org /10.2105/AJPH.2019.305015.

6. Interviewee in discussion with the author's research team, Puerto Rico, April 17, 2019. Audio on file with the author.

7. Kishore et al., "Mortality in Puerto Rico after Hurricane Maria."

8. Naomi Klein, "Puerto Ricans and Ultrarich 'Puertopians' Are Locked in a Pitched Struggle over How to Remake the Island," *The Intercept*, March 20, 2018, https://theintercept.com/2018/03/20/puerto-rico-hurricane -maria-recovery/.

9. "Public Utility Regulatory Policies Act," Pub. L. No. 95–617, 92 Stat. 3117 (1978). PURPA required utilities to buy power from any independent company that would sell power to the utility for less than the utility would spend to produce power with its own generators. Some regions of the United States, such as the Mountain West and the Southeast, are still dominated by vertically integrated utilities (see US Environmental Protection Agency, "U.S. Electricity Grid and Markets," https://www.epa.gov/greenpower/us-electricity-grid-markets).

10. On June 19, 1997, Pacific Gas & Electric (PG&E) was convicted of 739 counts of criminal negligence and was fined $24 million. (See Complaint made in Ellen and Cynthia Amador v. PG&E).

11. Complaint in Quammen, Smith, Bell et al. v. PG&E Corp., No. CGC-18-571281 (San Francsisco County Superior Court, 2018).

12. Matthias Gafni, "PG&E transmission line eyed in Camp Fire had collapsed during 2012 storm," *The Mercury News*, November 19, 2018, https://www.mercurynews.com/2018/11/19/pge-transmission-line-eyed-in-camp-fire-had-collapsed-during-2012-storm/.

13. Complaint in Quammen, Smith, Bell et al. v. PG&E Corp.; Ellen and Cynthia Amador v. PG&E Corp.; "SONOMA COUNTY / PG&E to Pay $5 Million—Fire Burned Vineyard," *SFGate*, May 21, 1999, https://www.sfgate.com/news/article/SONOMA-COUNTY-PG-E-to-Pay-5-Million-Fire-2929795.php.

14. One excluded example is the 2004 Power Fire, caused when a PG&E contractor left a cigarette burning on the ground while clearing vegetation. This rather ironic example illustrates a case when PG&E actually attempted to maintain the safety of the grid. The fire burned more than 17,000 acres of the Eldorado National Forest and took seventeen days and $8.46 million to suppress. (Complaint in Quammen, Smith, Bell et al. v. PG&E Corp.; Will Kane, "PG&E Contractor Settles Fire Case," *SFGate*, June 6, 2013, https://www.sfgate.com/news/article/PG-amp-E-contractor-settles-fire-case-4584565.php.)

15. PG&E, "Pacific Gas and Electric Company Amended 2019 Wildfire Safety Plan," February 6, 2019.

16. Ivan Penn, "'This Is Not Hard': PG&E Gets an Earful over Its Blackout," *New York Times*, October 18, 2019, sec. Business, https://www.nytimes.com/2019/10/18/business/energy-environment/pge-blackout-california.html.

17. Thomas Fuller and Tim Arango, "Fears of More Extreme Weather as Kincade Fire Swells," *New York Times*, October 28, 2019, sec. U.S., https://www.nytimes.com/2019/10/28/us/getty-fire-california.html.

18. Steven Weissman, "Turning Off the Lights in California," *New York Times*, October 14, 2019, sec. Opinion, https://www.nytimes.com/2019/10/14/opinion/pg-and-e-shutdown.html.

19. Diana Hernández and Stephen Bird, "Energy Burden and the Need for Integrated Low-Income Housing and Energy Policy," *Poverty and Public Policy* 2, no. 4 (2010): 5–25, https://doi.org/10.2202/1944-2858.1095.

20. Thomas Fuller, "For the Most Vulnerable, California Blackouts 'Can Be Life or Death,'" *New York Times*, October 10, 2019, sec. U.S., https://www.nytimes.com/2019/10/10/us/california-power-outage.html.

21. James Glanz and Brad Plumer, "In a High-Tech State, Blackouts Are a Low-Tech Way to Prevent Fires," *New York Times*, October 12, 2019, sec. Business, https://www.nytimes.com/2019/10/12/business/power-blackouts-california-microgrids.html.

22. J. R. Minkel, "The 2003 Northeast Blackout—Five Years Later," *Scientific American*, August 13, 2008, https://www.scientificamerican.com/article/2003-blackout-five-years-later/.

23. "Energy Policy Act of 2005," Pub. L. No. 109–58, 42 U.S.C. 15801 (2005). The law states that, for "purposes of this paragraph, the term 'net metering service' means service to an electric customer under which electric energy generated by that electric customer from an eligible on-site generating facility and delivered to the local distribution facilities may be used to offset electric energy provided by the electric utility to the electric consumer during the applicable billing period."

24. For example, North Carolina adopted a 35 percent personal tax credit for renewable energy installations in 1977. See D. Steward et al., "The Effectiveness of State-Level Policies on Solar Market Development in Different State Contexts," National Renewable Energy Laboratory, February 2014.

25. Richard D. Cudahy, "PURPA: The Intersection of Competition and Regulatory Policy," *Energy Law Journal* 16, no. 2 (1995): 421, 425.

26. Richard F. Hirsh, "PURPA: The Spur to Competition and Utility Restructuring," *Electricity Journal* 12, no. 7 (August 1, 1999): 62, https://doi.org/10.1016/S1040-6190(99)00060-3.

27. Solar Energy Industries Association, "The Public Utility Regulatory

Policies Act of 1978," September 2018, https://www.seia.org/sites/default /files/2018-09/SEIA-PURPA-101-Factsheet-2018-Sept.pdf.

28. James W. Stoutenborough and Matthew Beverlin, "Encouraging Pollution-Free Energy: The Diffusion of State Net Metering Policies," *Social Science Quarterly* 89, no. 5 (2008): 1232, https://doi.org/10.1111/j.1540 -6237.2008.00571.x; Ryan Wiser et al., "The Experience with Renewable Portfolio Standards in the United States," *Electricity Journal* 20, no. 4 (May 1, 2007): 9, https://doi.org/10.1016/j.tej.2007.03.009.

29. Boris R. Lukanov and Elena M. Krieger, "Distributed Solar and Environmental Justice: Exploring the Demographic and Socio-Economic Trends of Residential PV Adoption in California," *Energy Policy* 134 (November 1, 2019): 110935, https://doi.org/10.1016/j.enpol.2019.110935.

30. North Carolina Clean Energy Technology Center, "Programs," accessed May 7, 2020, https://programs.dsireusa.org/system/program.

31. Ran Fu, David Feldman, and Robert Margolis, "U.S. Solar Photovoltaic System Cost Benchmark: Q1 2018," National Renewable Energy Laboratory, November 2018.

32. Deborah Sunter, Sergio Castellanos, and Daniel Kammen, "Disparities in Rooftop Photovoltaics Deployment in the United States by Race and Ethnicity," *Nature Sustainability* 2 (January 10, 2019), https://doi.org/10 .1038/s41893-018-0204-z.

33. Sunter, Castellanos, and Kammen, "Disparities in Rooftop Photovoltaics Deployment."

34. An analysis by Common Cause lists the Koch brothers and several oil and gas companies among a list of corporations that support ALEC's work. Jay Riestenberg, "Who Still Funds ALEC?," Common Cause, https:// www.commoncause.org/democracy-wire/who-still-funds-alec/.

35. "Application of the Arizona Public Service Company before the Arizona Corporation Commission in Docket E-01345A-13-0248," July 12, 2013, 4.

36. The US Department of Energy describes a prosumer as "someone who both produces and consumes energy—a shift made possible, in part, due to the rise of new connected technologies and the steady increase of more renewable power like solar and wind onto our electric grid." Sarah Harman, "Consumer vs. Prosumer: What's the Difference?," US Department of Energy, May 11, 2017, https://www.energy.gov/eere/articles/consumer -vs-prosumer-whats-difference.

37. North Carolina Clean Energy Technology Center, "The 50 States of Solar: 2019 Policy Review and Q4 Quarterly Report," January 2020.

38. "Application of the Arizona Public Service Company before the Arizona Corporation Commission in Docket E-01345A-13-0248," 8.

39. "Application of the Arizona Public Service Company before the Arizona Corporation Commission in Docket E-01345A-13-0248," 8.

40. Tom Tanton, "Reforming Net Metering: Providing a Bright and Equitable Future," American Legislative Exchange Council, March 2014, https://www.alec.org/app/uploads/2015/12/2014-Net-Metering-reform-web.pdf, 17.

41. "Application of the Arizona Public Service Company before the Arizona Corporation Commission in Docket E-01345A-13-0248," 9.

42. Peter Kind, "Disruptive Challenges: Financial Implications and Strategic Responses to a Changing Retail Electric Business," Edison Electric Institute, January 2013, https://www.ourenergypolicy.org/wp-content/uploads/2013/09/disruptivechallenges-1.pdf.

43. Tom Tanton, "Reforming Net Metering: Providing a Bright and Equitable Future," 2 (my emphasis).

44. Ivan Penn, "N.A.A.C.P. Tells Local Chapters: Don't Let Energy Industry Manipulate You," *New York Times*, January 5, 2020, https://www.nytimes.com/2020/01/05/business/energy-environment/naacp-utility-donations.html.

45. New York State Energy Research & Development Authority, "The Value Stack," https://www.nyserda.ny.gov/All-Programs/Programs/NY-Sun/Contractors/Value-of-Distributed-Energy-Resources.

46. "Intervenor's Fees and Expenses," Cal. Pub. Util. Code § 1801.3 (2017); Charlie Harak, John Howat, and Olivia Wein, "A Consumer's Guide to Intervening in State Public Utility Proceedings," National Consumer Law Center, March 2004.

Chapter 5. Community Energy: The Devil Is in the Details

1. US Geological Survey, Lawrence Berkeley National Laboratory, and American Wind Energy Association, "U.S. Wind Turbine Database," April 2020, https://eerscmap.usgs.gov/uswtdb/viewer/#9.37/21.4635/-157.8139.

2. Elemental Excelerator, "NextEra Energy Merges with Hawaiian Electric,"

CleanTechnica, December 5, 2014, https://cleantechnica.com/2014/12/05 /nextera-energy-merges-hawaiian-electric-gains-foothold-nations-best -energy-test-bed/.

3. Ivan Penn, "Florida's Utilities Keep Homeowners from Making the Most of Solar Power," *New York Times,* July 7, 2019, sec. Business, https://www .nytimes.com/2019/07/07/business/energy-environment/florida-solar -power.html; Dave Anderson, "Real Solar Cost Shift: Utilities Force Customers to Subsidize Attacks on Solar," *Energy and Policy Institute* (blog), November 4, 2016, https://www.energyandpolicy.org/real-solar-cost-shift -subsidized-attacks-on-rooftop-solar/.

4. Krisnawati Suryanata, "Products from Paradise: The Social Construction of Hawaii Crops," *Agriculture and Human Values* 17, no. 2 (June 1, 2000): 181–89, https://doi.org/10.1023/A:1007617403517.

5. In reality, the number may be closer to ten days. See "A Bill for an Act Relating to Food Self-Sufficiency," H.B. 2703 (2012), which states that Hawai'i imports about 92 percent of its food and only has enough produce for ten days at any one time. https://www.capitol.hawaii.gov/session 2012/Bills/HB2703_HD2_pdf.

6. Carlos Andrade, "A Hawaiian Geography or A Geography of Hawai'i?," in *I Ulu I Ka 'Aina: Land* (Honolulu: University of Hawai'i Press, 2014), 8.

7. Kawika B. Winter et al., "The Moku System: Managing Biocultural Resources for Abundance within Social-Ecological Regions in Hawai'i," *Sustainability* 10, no. 10 (October 2018): 2, https://doi.org/10.3390 /su10103554.

8. Winter et al., "The Moku System," 6.

9. Winter et al., "The Moku System," 8.

10. "Final Environmental Assessment, Finding of No Significant Impact: Statewide Programmatic General Permit and Programmatic Agreement for the Restoration, Repair, Maintenance and Reconstruction of Traditional Hawaiian Fishpond Systems across Hawai'i" (Department of Land and Natural Resources, October 2013), 17.

11. "Final Environmental Assessment," 4.

12. "Final Environmental Assessment," 4.

13. "Hawai'i Act 100" (2015). "While residential solar energy use has grown dramatically across the State in recent years, many residents and businesses are currently unable to directly participate in renewable energy

generation because of their location, building type, access to the electricity grid, and other impediments."

14. North Carolina Clean Energy Technology Center, "The 50 States of Solar: 2019 Policy Review and Q4 Quarterly Report," January 2020.

15. Warren Leon et al., "Solar with Justice: Strategies for Powering Up Under-Resourced Communities and Growing an Inclusive Solar Market," Clean Energy States Alliance, December 2019, 15 (emphasis in original).

16. Leon et al., "Solar with Justice," 15.

17. Leon et al., "Solar with Justice," 15.

18. Herman Trabish, "17% of Hawaiian Electric Customers Now Have Rooftop Solar," Utility Dive, accessed March 10, 2020, https://www.utilitydive.com/news/17-of-hawaiian-electric-customers-now-have-rooftop-solar/413014/; Hawai'i Act 100.

19. Hawai'i Act 100.

20. North Carolina Clean Energy Technology Center, "Business Energy Investment Tax Credit," February 13, 2020, https://programs.dsireusa.org/system/program/detail/658.

21. Public Utilities Commission of the State of Hawai'i, "Decision and Order No. 35137" In Docket No. 2015-0389 (2018).

22. Arroyo Seco Consulting, "IO Update on CBRE Program Phase I," July 25, 2019.

23. Hawaii State Energy Office, "Hawaii Energy Facts & Figures," July 2019, https://energy.hawaii.gov/wp-content/uploads/2019/07/2019-FF_Final.pdf; Scott Seu, Hawaiian Electric Companies Overview: Briefing for World Bank, Hawaiian Electric Company, May 23, 2016, https://www.esmap.org/sites/esmap.org/files/Hawaiian%20Electric%20Company%20-%20Overview_web.pdf.

24. Jason Coughlin et al., "A Guide to Community Shared Solar: Utility, Private, and Nonprofit Project Development," May 2012, https://www.nrel.gov/docs/fy12osti/54570.pdf, 6.

25. Coughlin et al., "A Guide to Community Shared Solar."

26. John Farrell, "Why Minnesota's Community Solar Program Is the Best," Institute for Local Self-Reliance, February 24, 2020, https://ilsr.org/minnesotas-community-solar-program/.

27. Timothy DenHerder-Thomas et al., "Equitable Community Solar: Policy

and Program Guidance for Community Solar Programs that Promote Racial and Economic Equity," Institute for Local Self-Reliance, February 2020, https://ilsr.org/wp-content/uploads/2020/02/Equitable-Commun ity-Solar-Report.pdf, 5.

Chapter 6. Access to Capital: A Way to End Solar Segregation

1. Mikel González-Eguino, "Energy Poverty: An Overview," *Renewable and Sustainable Energy Reviews* 47 (2015): 377–85, https://doi.org/10.1016/j .rser.2015.03.013.

2. Lakshman Guruswamy, "Energy Poverty," *Annual Review of Environment and Resources* 36, no. 1 (2011): 139–61, https://doi.org/10.1146/annurev -environ-040610-090118.

3. Diana Hernández and Stephen Bird, "Energy Burden and the Need for Integrated Low-Income Housing and Energy Policy," *Poverty and Public Policy* 2, no. 4 (2010): 5–25, https://doi.org/10.2202/1944-2858.1095.

4. Fisher, Sheehan & Colton, "Home Energy Affordability Gap," May 2013, http://www.homeenergyaffordabilitygap.com/.

5. Adam Chandler, "Where the Poor Spend More Than 10 Percent of Their Income on Energy," *The Atlantic*, June 8, 2016, https://www.theatlantic .com/business/archive/2016/06/energy-poverty-low-income-households /486197/.

6. Fisher, Sheehan & Colton, "Affordability Gap Data: Texas," Home Energy Affordability Gap, April 2019, http://www.homeenergyaffordabilitygap .com/03a_affordabilityData.html.

7. Office of Community Services, "LIHEAP Fact Sheet," November 16, 2018, https://www.acf.hhs.gov/ocs/resource/liheap-fact-sheet-0.

8. Tony G. Reames, "Improving the Effectiveness of Federal Energy Assis- tance for Low-Income Households," Scholars Strategy Network, January 1, 2017, https://scholars.org/contribution/improving-effectiveness-federal -energy-assistance-low-income-households.

9. Sarah Crowley, "Directing Help Towards the Vulnerable: Joining Penn- sylvania's SNAP and Energy Assistance Applications," Roosevelt Institute, 2018, http://rooseveltinstitute.org/wp-content/uploads/2018/05/Roose velt_10-Ideas_Environment_Directing-Help-Towards-the-Vulnerable .pdf.

10. Hernández and Bird, "Energy Burden."

11. Massachusetts Department of Public Utilities, "Billing and Termination Procedures" (n.d.).

12. Talis Shelbourne, "What You Need to Know before the Energy Moratorium Starts Nov. 1," *Milwaukee Journal Sentinel*, October 30, 2019, https://www.jsonline.com/story/news/local/milwaukee/2019/10/30/what-you-need-know-before-energy-moratorium-starts-nov-1/3840223002/.

13. US Department of Health and Human Services, "State Disconnection Policies," accessed March 13, 2020, https://liheapch.acf.hhs.gov/Disconnect/disconnect.htm.

14. US Department of Health and Human Services, "State Disconnection Policies."

15. Jeremy S. Hoffman, Vivek Shandas, and Nicholas Pendleton, "The Effects of Historical Housing Policies on Resident Exposure to Intra-Urban Heat: A Study of 108 US Urban Areas," *Climate* 8, no. 1 (January 2020): 12, https://doi.org/10.3390/cli8010012.

16. Rachel Cluett, Jennifer Amann, and Sodavy Ou, "Building Better Energy Efficiency Programs for Low-Income Households" (Washington, DC: American Council for an Energy-Efficient Economy, March 2016), https://www.aceee.org/sites/default/files/publications/researchreports/a1601.pdf.

17. An American Council for an Energy-Efficiency Economy report cites "some type of health, safety, moisture, durability, and/or structural issue," Cluett, Amann, and Ou, "Building Better Energy Efficiency Programs," 13.

18. Cluett, Amann, and Ou, "Building Better Energy Efficiency Programs," 14.

19. Boris R. Lukanov and Elena M. Krieger, "Distributed Solar and Environmental Justice: Exploring the Demographic and Socio-Economic Trends of Residential PV Adoption in California," *Energy Policy* 134 (November 1, 2019): 110935, https://doi.org/10.1016/j.enpol.2019.110935; Deborah Sunter, Sergio Castellanos, and Daniel Kammen, "Disparities in Rooftop Photovoltaics Deployment in the United States by Race and Ethnicity," *Nature Sustainability* 2 (January 10, 2019), https://doi.org/10.1038/s41893-018-0204-z.

20. Jason Coughlin et al., "A Guide to Community Shared Solar: Utility, Private, and Nonprofit Project Development," May 2012, https://www.nrel.gov/docs/fy12osti/54570.pdf, 4.

21. Coughlin et al., "A Guide to Community Shared Solar," 4.

22. Connecticut Green Bank, "Comprehensive Annual Financial Report," 2019, ii.

23. Connecticut Green Bank, "Comprehensive Annual Financial Report," ii.

24. Connecticut Green Bank, "Comprehensive Annual Financial Report," ii.

25. Bryan Garcia, "Progress Report on the Connecticut Green Bank Residential Solar Investment Program," January 11, 2019, 3.

26. Connecticut Green Bank, "Comprehensive Plan," July 2019, 9.

27. Connecticut Green Bank, "Sharing Solar Benefits: Reaching Households of Underserved Communities of Color in Connecticut," May 2019, 3; Connecticut Green Bank, "Comprehensive Plan," 11.

28. Connecticut Green Bank, "Sharing Solar Benefits: Reaching Households of Underserved Communities of Color in Connecticut," 3.

29. Garcia, "Progress Report on the Connecticut Green Bank Residential Solar Investment Program."

30. Garcia, "Progress Report on the Connecticut Green Bank Residential Solar Investment Program."

31. Leon et al., "Solar with Justice: Strategies for Powering Up Under-Resourced Communities and Growing an Inclusive Solar Market," Clean Energy States Alliance, December 2019, 58.

32. North Carolina Clean Energy Technology Center, "Local Option—Commercial PACE Financing," DSIRE, accessed March 20, 2020, https://programs.dsireusa.org/system/program/detail/5321.

33. Connecticut Green Bank, "Solar Power Purchase Agreement," 2017, http://ctgreenbank.com/wp-content/uploads/2017/02/Solar-PPA-program-sheet.pdf.

34. Connecticut Green Bank, "Green Bonds Us," 2019, https://ctgreenbank.com/wp-content/uploads/2019/12/AR-FY19-layout-single-pages-1.pdf.

35. Connecticut Green Bank, "Green Bonds Us."

36. Connecticut Green Bank, "Comprehensive Plan."

37. New York Public Service Commission, "Order Establishing New York Green Bank and Providing Initial Capitalization" in Case 13-M-0412, December 19, 2013.

38. New York Public Service Commission, "Order Establishing New York Green Bank and Providing Initial Capitalization," 1.

39. New York Public Service Commission, "Order Establishing New York Green Bank and Providing Initial Capitalization," 16.

40. Hawaii Department of Business, Economic Development and Tourism, "Hawaii Green Infrastructure Authority: Annual Report to the Governor and Legislature," December 20, 2019, 5.

41. Hawaii Department of Business, Economic Development and Tourism, "Hawaii Green Infrastructure Authority," 5.

42. Hawaii Department of Business, Economic Development and Tourism, "Hawaii Green Infrastructure Authority," 12.

43. Patricia Tummons, "Much-Touted Green Energy Program Falls Far Short of the Hype," March 5, 2015, https://www.civilbeat.org/2015/03/much -touted-green-energy-program-falls-far-short-of-the-hype/; Tom Yamachika, "GEMS as a Target for Raiding?," Tax Foundation of Hawaii, August 22, 2016, https://www.tfhawaii.org/wordpress/blog/2016/08 /gems-as-a-target-for-raiding/.

44. Hawaii Public Utilities Commission, "Order No. 34930: Amending Decision and Order No. 32318 by Changing the Priority of Uses of GEMS Program Loan Repayments" in Docket No. 2014-0135 October 26, 2017. Order 34930 says that "3% of GEMS funds" were loaned three years into the program.

45. Hawaii Public Utilities Commission, "Order No. 34930."

46. "GEMS Financing Program," accessed March 24, 2020, https://gems .hawaii.gov.

47. Diana Hernández and Stephen Bird, "Energy Burden and the Need for Integrated Low-Income Housing and Energy Policy," *Poverty and Public Policy* 2, no. 4 (2010): 12, https://doi.org/10.2202/1944-2858.1095; Feeding America, "In Short Supply: American Families Struggle to Secure Everyday Essentials," 2013, https://www.feedingamerica.org/sites/default /files/research/in-short-supply/in-short-supply-executive.pdf.

48. I attended a closed meeting at which a frontline advocate made mention of this approach, but because it would be such a departure from standard regulatory practice, she declined to go on record with the recommendation.

49. Richard Rothstein, *Color of Law* (New York: Liveright, 2017).

50. Rothstein, *Color of Law.*

51. Feeding America, "In Short Supply."

52. Forrest Watkins, "The EnergyScore: For a More Inclusive Solar Future," *Solstice Community Solar* (blog), February 2, 2018, https://solstice.us /solstice-blog/energyscore-more-inclusive-solar-future/.

53. Watkins, "The EnergyScore."

54. Solar Energy Industries Association, "Inclusive Solar Financing for Low Income Solar," December 12, 2018, https://www.seia.org/sites/default /files/2018-12/Inclusive%20Solar%20Financing%20for%20Low%20 Income%20Solar_12.12.18_Master%20Deck.pdf.

55. United States Census, "QuickFacts: Milwaukee County, Wisconsin," 2019, https://www.census.gov/quickfacts/milwaukeecountywisconsin.

56. Environmental Collaboration Office, "Property Eligibility," City of Milwaukee, accessed March 24, 2020, https://city.milwaukee.gov/me2 /Homeowners/Property-Eligibility.htm#.XnpJ2tNKjOR.

57. Environmental Collaboration Office, "Property Eligibility."

58. Environmental Collaboration Office, "Property Eligibility."

59. Leon et al., "Solar with Justice," 54.

60. Shalanda H. Baker, "Anti-Resilience: A Roadmap for Transformational Justice within the Energy System," *Harvard Civil Rights-Civil Liberties Law Review* 54, no. 1 (Winter 2019): 40.

61. Baker, "Anti-Resilience," 40.

Conclusion: Revolutionary Power

1. Henry Curtis, "State of Hawaiʻi Energy Policy—Part 1: From Climate Change to Microgrids, Carbon Taxes and Beyond, Ililani Media, February 25, 2019, https://www.esmap.org/sites/esmap.org/files/Hawaiian%20 Electric%20Company%20-%20Overview_web.pdf.

2. CDC, "Coronavirus Disease 2019 (COVID-19) Situation Summary," Centers for Disease Control and Prevention, April 19, 2020, https://www .cdc.gov/coronavirus/2019-ncov/cases-updates/summary.html.

3. Xiao Wu et al., "Exposure to Air Pollution and COVID-19 Mortality in the United States" (Harvard T. H. Chan School of Public Health, April 5, 2020), https://projects.iq.harvard.edu/files/covid-pm/files/pm_and_covid _mortality.pdf.

4. Wu et al., "Exposure to Air Pollution and COVID-19 Mortality in the United States."

5. Wu et al., "Exposure to Air Pollution and COVID-19 Mortality in the United States."

6. IPCC, "Summary for Policymakers," Global Warming of 1.5°C. An IPCC Special Report on the Impacts of Global Warming of 1.5°C above Pre-Industrial Levels and Related Global Greenhouse Gas Emission Pathways, in the Context of Strengthening the Global Response to the Threat of Climate Change, Sustainable Development, and Efforts to Eradicate Poverty, 2018, https://www.ipcc.ch/sr15/.

About the Author

Dana Smith

Shalanda H. Baker is a professor of law, public policy, and urban affairs at Northeastern University. She has spent more than a decade conducting research on the equity dimensions of the global transition away from fossil fuel energy to cleaner energy resources. She teaches courses on renewable energy development, energy justice, and environmental law. In 2015, she was awarded a 2016–2017 Fulbright–García Robles grant to explore Mexico's energy reform, climate change, and Indigenous rights.

Before joining Northeastern's faculty, Baker spent three years as an associate professor of law at the William S. Richardson School of Law, University of Hawai'i, where she was the founding director of the Energy Justice Program. Prior to that, she served on the faculty at the University of San Francisco School of Law. She holds a bachelor of science degree in political science from the United States Air Force Academy, a juris doctor from Northeastern University School of Law, and an LLM from the University of Wisconsin School of Law, where she also served as a William H. Hastie fellow. Immediately after law school, before working as a corporate and project finance attorney in both the Boston and Tokyo offices of the law firm of Bingham McCutchen, Baker clerked for Associate Justice Roderick Ireland of the Massachusetts Supreme Judicial Court. Baker is also a veteran and former Air Force officer who fought to end the military's "Don't Ask, Don't Tell" policy.

She is the author of over a dozen articles, book chapters, and essays on renewable energy law, policy, and development. She is the cofounder and codirector of the Initiative for Energy Justice (www.iejusa.org), an organization committed to providing technical law and policy support to communities on the front lines of climate change. She also serves on the Massachusetts Energy Facilities Siting Board, the Massachusetts Global Warming Solutions Act Implementation Advisory Committee Climate Justice Working Group, the Board of the Solutions Project, and the Board of the Clean Energy Group.

Index